STUPID FAC

For a complete list of Management Books 2000 titles,
visit our website on www.mb2000.com

STUPID FACTOR

**Find success with your start-up
by avoiding the critical mistakes entrepreneurs make**

Peter Jump

with Smart Thinking from
Prof David Birchall
of Henley Management College

Cover photograph by KA Blendulf

2000

To Edith, Anneli and Kerstin

First published in 2006 by Management Books 2000 Ltd
Forge House, Limes Road
Kemble, Cirencester
Gloucestershire, GL7 6AD, UK
Tel: 0044 (0) 1285 771441
Fax: 0044 (0) 1285 771055
E-mail: info@mb2000.com
Web: www.mb2000.com

Printed and bound in Great Britain by www.webspeedbooks.com

British Library Cataloguing in Publication Data is available
ISBN 1-85252-520-7

Contents

Foreword

In many ways there has never been a better time to start a business. Quite apart from very favourable economic conditions – continuous growth, strong consumer spending and low inflation – there is an unprecedented amount of help readily available for would-be business people. This ranges from the training and advice provided by such organisations as Business Link to financial assistance from bodies like the Prince's Trust, the Regional Development Agencies and the increasing number of business angel networks. It has now been clearly recognised that new businesses, especially those with high growth potential, are central to the continued vitality of the country's economy. That means entrepreneurs are now seen, quite rightly, as important people who should be given the best possible chance for success – for everyone's sake!

But is all this encouragement and support actually having any effect? All the signs are that it is, with new businesses starting up in huge numbers each year. Indeed, small and medium-sized enterprises (SMEs) are now, collectively, the UK's biggest employer.

At Henley Management College we have certainly seen an increase in enquiries from those seeking to prepare themselves for life managing a start-up. As it happens, the College has for many years included an entrepreneurial element in its MBA programmes. But now we are seeing a growing demand from senior corporate executives, many already with MBAs, for courses specifically tailored to help them make the transition from working in big companies to running small – but ambitious – new ventures. The entrepreneurial bug seems to be catching, and not just amongst brash whiz-kids wanting to be the next Branson or Gates.

However, all this help and encouragement for start-ups doesn't negate the fact that there are some major challenges ahead for UK businesses. Most notably, new firms now need to think longer and harder than ever before about where their competition will be coming from. Few can now afford to just look in their immediate location; they also need to think about the threat posed by businesses in developing countries such as India and China. And it's not just manufacturers that need to worry – even service providers, most notably those in the IT sector, now have to look over their shoulder at the emerging economies.

New businesses, therefore, need to prepare as never before to fight off competition. This includes planning how they can move as quickly as possible from supplying a 'commodity' product or generic service to higher value work. And many businesses now have to think how they can build additional services around their core offering in order to achieve the required levels of profit and growth.

When doing all this planning, start-ups should make sure to take maximum advantage of being based in one of the world's longest established and most vibrant capitalist economies. By this I mean exploiting the immense wealth of business knowledge and experience that surrounds us through such means as networking, mentoring and coaching, and by seeking out investors who are able to provide not just money but also guidance and sound advice. Certainly, don't take the innate benefits you gain from being based in the UK (yes, there definitely are benefits!) for granted.

Another challenge that needs to be overcome is the current talent shortage, especially regarding employees with scientific or technical skills. Smaller companies, in particular, find it difficult to attract, motivate and keep these high quality people as they may not be able to offer the salaries, working environments and security of major corporations. This is compounded by the fact that employees in smaller companies need to be willing to get involved with all areas of the business, and not just their particular specialism. All the signs are that the talent crisis will get considerably worse before it gets better, and you need to know how you will handle it.

A further critical issue is the quality of leadership and management in start-ups (and indeed all SMEs). In other words, are you yourself up to the job of running a business? Henley's own research has shown this is definitely a source of concern for many entrepreneurs, and one that needs to be properly addressed in order to fulfil a new company's includes serial entrepreneurs who have been previously involved in a string of successful start-ups.) Worse still, they were often quite aware that they were doing something they shouldn't have been, but went ahead and did it anyway. Why?

An inflated sense of their own abilities can be one reason, along with a belief that with energy and determination there is no difficulty they can't overcome. Another is expedience (although in many cases laziness might be a better word), with corners being cut to save time and effort. Or it may be that they learnt the wrong lessons from a previous business, where they took a chance by doing something that wasn't best practice and got away with it – but find they aren't so lucky second time around.

Then there's the phenomenon of wilful ignorance, which I came across repeatedly in my research – entrepreneurs know they don't have the knowledge and experience they need when they start, but think this can be picked up as they go along. They may even think that their ignorance is some sort of virtue, providing a 'fresh perspective' which enables them to outwit their more knowledgeable and experienced competitors. Only rarely does this prove the case.

I accept that sometimes I will be stating things that are pretty obvious, even to those who have never run their own business before. But in a sense that is one of the basic purposes of the book: to make sure entrepreneurs, whether new or experienced, don't let the excitement of turning their ideas into working businesses lead them to lose sight of what is good business practice. If all this book does is pull you back from doing something that your business instincts have already told you is a bad idea, then it has done its job.

Who is this book for?

Stupid Factor is for anyone starting (or even thinking about starting) any kind of new business. Whether it's setting up as a computer consultant or self-employed domestic plumber, opening a clothes shop or Italian restaurant, or launching a hi-tech company that will rival Google and Microsoft, Stupid Factor can help your business get off to a flying start. At the very least, it will steer you around the pitfalls that take out 50 per cent of companies in their first three years of trading.

Stupid Factor is also of great value to managers of established firms keen to further develop their businesses with minimum risk and maximum effectiveness. That's because all companies – even the biggest – need to beware of making 'unforced errors' when they decide to grow rapidly or change direction. Examples of businesses that failed to appreciate that include GEC with its ill-fated move into telecommunications, and Motorola with its disastrous satellite venture, Iridium.

How to use this book

I have tried to encapsulate the common mistakes and misconceptions of entrepreneurs in statements I've called Stupid Factors – for example:

> **Setting up and running a business is easier than working for someone else.**

Under each of these you will find a concise explanation as to why these are bad ideas. Along with the statements there are information boxes providing explanations, advice and smart tips on the business issues you will have to deal with as you start and develop your venture. Each main chapter deals with a key aspect of setting up a successful business, and together they provide a road map for getting from a vague aspiration or hazy idea to a thriving enterprise.

As you progress through *Stupid Factor,* you will also find real-life Start-up Stories, which roughly relate to the main chapters they follow. With each one, I have attempted to highlight as much as possible the universal business issues that were encountered by the entrepreneurs. So, even if a story is about a business that is wholly unrelated to your start-up, you should still find something of value in it.

The most obvious way in which you can use this book is as a common sense, step-by-step guide to creating your own start-up, in which case you will probably want to read all of it before you start making any big decisions or spending any money. But what you can also do, once you are in business, is use it as a reference manual to help you in your day-to-day decision making. In particular, when you feel the urge to do something stupid, look in the relevant main chapter and read the Stupid Factor which closest matches what you are thinking of doing. Such urges will usually be associated with:

- expediency (*'I'm sure we'll get away with simply...'*)
- laziness (*'I can't be bothered...'*)
- extreme cost saving (*'We can save lots of cash if we just...'*)
- quick money
- blind faith (*'Let's hope that...'*)
- arrogance
- lack of confidence
- unrealistic expectations
- uncalculated risk taking (*'Let's take a gamble that...'*).

You should also take a closer look at the various case studies. Hopefully, this will pull you back from the brink of doing something that you'll come to regret only too soon.

Smart thinking

David Birchall is a leading expert on SME leadership. (SME – Small and Medium-sized Enterprises – is a term which includes everything from one-man bands to companies employing a hundred or so people. Your start-up will almost certainly be an SME to begin with.) He is also one of the longest serving professors at the world-renowned Henley Management College, and kindly supplied the author with a plentiful supply of well-observed comment and advice for entrepreneurs.

Case studies and start-up stories

All of these are based on real businesses, although identifying details have been altered for some of them. A few involve entrepreneurs who made smart moves that others might benefit from trying, while the rest tell the tales of businesses that blundered into Stupid Factors, sometimes resulting in the firm being forced out of business. Motorcycle Voyager Ltd (**Start-up Stories: Publish and Be Damned,** page 181) is the most stunning example of the latter, and its story is, sadly, pretty much all true. In fact, working at that company provided me with the inspiration for *Stupid Factor*.

Acknowledgements

This book would not be half so informative were it not for the many people who freely gave their help, usually by allowing themselves to be subjected to scatological interrogation by the author. It was through these interviews that I not only came up with ideas to include in the book, but also had many of my own assumptions regarding starting and managing a business either confirmed or challenged. Those to whom my thanks are due include: Chris Price of ICON Corporate Finance, work psychologist David Mathews, Pascale Bennett of Stowford Framing, Toby Chapman-Dawe, Ian Roberts, Adam Wurf, Steve Rosier of BACH Homes, Fraser MacKay of Barclays Bank, Eva Fernandez of BORN, Ray Hurcombe of Finance Wales, Phil Davies of telescratch, Jeremy Holt of Clark Holt Commercial Solicitors, Peter Maxwell and Nick Sturge of SETsquared (University of Bristol), Harold Beirne, Samantha Cooke, Chris with the great cars at Classic Car Club (Bristol), Malcolm Gregory and Chris Inson of Withy King solicitors, Greg Wood of Connect 360, Rohan Master, Jessica Hawker – The MathMagician, Roger Croft and Carole Sheppard of Entrepreneurs South West (Bath University) and Prof David Birchall and the rest of the team at Henley Management College. I would particularly like to thank my fiancée, Anneli Blendulf, for her tireless support throughout the writing of *Stupid Factor* and her merciless editing of the original draft.

1

All About You

The most important factor in the success of your new business is you – the person you are is more important even than the idea behind the business (no matter how brilliantly original that may be) or the amount of money you have to spend on it. That's not to say you won't succeed unless you match up to a blueprint for the perfect entrepreneur (the genius of Gates, the savvy of Sugar and the beard of Branson). In fact, the good news is that many very ordinary people, who haven't been blessed with any exceptional gifts (or facial hair), have had tremendous success running their own start-ups. But what you do need is a clear understanding of who you are, where your strengths and weaknesses lie, and how all this relates to setting up in business.

To help you do this we'll examine some fundamental misconceptions you may have about running a new venture, and also your motivation for abandoning straightforward employment. Simply wanting the freedom of not having a boss is at least as good a reason for starting a company as a desperate desire to make lots of money.

⚠️ **Setting up and running a business is easier than working for someone else.**

If this is really what you think, then like the soldiers who thought the First World War would be over by Christmas, you're in for a nasty surprise. Almost certainly, you will find yourself working longer and harder than you've ever done as an employee. You'll also be stretched, mentally if not physically, in ways you never imagined as you suddenly have to take on innumerable roles, few of which you'll be qualified for. Along with being the boss, also expect to be the secretary, bookkeeper, purchasing manager, salesperson and general labourer as well. And as for taking plenty of holidays and enjoying a normal social life, forget it. Fact is, when you start a company you've given birth to a hungry, screaming baby that'll demand all your time and energy from day one.

I'll hire people to do all the hard work, then sit back and watch the money pour in.

Sticking with the parenting analogy, taking on employees is like adopting a gang of unruly toddlers. That's not to say they'll poop in their pants and draw on the walls (but then again, who knows), but they are a responsibility that will only add to the demands on your time, energy and, in the short term at least, financial resources. By all means, take on employees if they are necessary for your business, but don't expect that doing so will leave you with more time to lean back and puff on your big cigar.

Working for yourself is how you get rich quick. That's what my mate Jim down the pub did six months ago and now he drives a Merc.

Many businesses make little, if any, money in their first year, so it's vital to have a long-term view. Even if your new business makes a decent profit from the start, you can still end up feeling skint five years down the line. That's because if you want your start-up to grow and be a real success, you'll need to put almost every penny you make back into it. Trust me, in a few weeks Jim will be trading down to a second-hand Renault Megane.

Starting my own business is a way to get out of the rat race and de-stress.

Whether it's a goat ranch in Wales, a web design agency in Manchester or an organic restaurant in London, don't see starting a business as a form of relaxation therapy. Instead, expect a new selection of stresses to keep you awake at night. As for getting you out of the rat race, becoming a business person simply puts you in a faster race with even bigger rats.

I'm damn good at my job in Megacorp plc, so I'm sure I can run my own company.

Don't assume that because you're a good employee you'll be good at running a business. As a wage slave, your role is probably well defined, with superiors telling you what to do. Even if you are a senior manager used to making strategic decisions and giving direction to others, chances are there is a team of secretaries, administrators and other managers backing you up. But as the boss of a start-up, you'll soon find yourself with responsibilities in areas you're totally unfamiliar with, and without the well-oiled administrative machine you're used to. Suddenly, that Employee of the Month award seems rather irrelevant.

Are you up to the challenge?

Most obviously, do you have the skills specifically required by the sort of business you are setting up? As a trivial example, you wouldn't open a carpentry workshop unless you were very skilled at woodwork. But what about opening a boutique? Many people wouldn't even consider that any skills, as such, were required to do this – but they'd be wrong. Can you arrange a window display that will draw in punters? And once customers are inside do you have the selling skills that will see someone who came in for a thong, leaving with a designer dress and a pair of shoes? If the answer isn't an unreserved 'yes' in key areas like this, then think about getting some training before you open shop.

Secondly, do you have the knowledge demanded by your chosen business? A plumber in Poland may have all the skills he needs to do his job, but if he wants to work in the UK he'll soon get into serious trouble without knowledge of local regulations and standard practices. Gaining the knowledge you need may be as trivial as reading a book, researching on the Internet or taking a night class, but whatever is required make sure you know what you need to know before you begin. Learning on the job is to be avoided as much as possible.

Now take a long look in the mirror and ask yourself if you have the personal qualities needed to successfully start a business. You must have energy, drive and ambition; be a doer who can focus on objectives and achieve them whatever the obstacles; a visionary who can anticipate the market; a leader who can take responsibility, make decisions and inspire those around you. You should also be able to take risks and have the mental robustness to keep going if things go wrong. It would also be very handy if you were organised, articulate and outgoing.

Not sure if you have a big helping of all these characteristics? Don't worry, few people do. You may, therefore, find it more useful to start with who you are rather than who you ought to be. Then you can plan how to work around your deficiencies, because simply thinking 'I can change' will not magically turn you overnight into the perfect person to run a business. Saying that, over time you should be able to make gradual, positive changes to the way you work. This will happen as you find that new ways of working – being more assertive or decisive, perhaps – actually make life easier for you. Ultimately, the more honest you are with yourself about yourself at the beginning, the better your chances of success in the long run.

Then there are factors to consider relating to your personal circumstances. Do you have the time to commit to a new venture? This could be a problem if you want to start a company without quitting your current job, or if you're a lone parent with childcare considerations. You should also think about your health and if this is likely to affect a new business (or be affected by the stress of going into business). Without the safety net of employee sick pay and colleagues who can take over your duties while you are absent, being ill when you are working for yourself can have dire financial consequences. Finally, will your partner be supportive, emotionally if not financially, when you ditch the steady income to pursue your entrepreneurial dream? If you think they won't be, then you really have some thinking to do.

CASE STUDY: The Zinger

Recently separated from her husband and with three young children to care for, Pascale Barrett needed to find a way to make ends meet – and quickly. Her solution was to set up a business she could manage from home, and the idea she hit upon for it was to manufacture and sell the Zinger. This was a hair accessory of her own invention which she believed would be particularly popular with young girls. It consisted of a strip of leather that was laced around a tress of hair to produce a sort of bondage ponytail.

After producing a few prototypes and testing them out on her target market, she soon found a local manufacturer, Clarks, willing to produce them for her. While hair accessories aren't something this well-known British company is usually associated with, it was willing to divert skilled staff from making leather shoes into putting together the leather Zingers. Pascale now had a reputable manufacturer as part of her team, which represented a major development for the business.

On top of that, she was able to secure a £5,000 grant from a government fund specifically intended to support manufacturing. Although she would later comment: *'I wish I'd asked for even more money – they never checked on me after I'd actually received the grant.'* All that was left to do now was to market the product, secure orders, then tell Clarks to swing into production. Did I say 'all'?

Pascale produced a basic brochure then started knocking on the doors of the national chain stores. Boots was soon interested, and at a meeting Pascale agreed a price for supplying the Zinger to this major retailer. The dream of financial security through a home-run business looked within her grasp. But a few days later she got a call from the buyer saying that Boots would only take the Zingers for a lower price – one that would eliminate all of Pascale's profit margin. She was left no option but to walk away from the deal.

Without a big retailer on board, distributing and selling the Zinger would now be a major struggle and involve approaching innumerable small retailers, which would take lots of time and effort. She could also have tried selling the accessories herself direct to consumers, at music festivals perhaps. But again, this would have taken time that she simply didn't have, given she had young children to look after. Her problems were compounded when local TV coverage of her Zingers alerted the authorities to the fact that one of their benefit claimants was also running a 'high-powered' manufacturing company. This resulted in her losing her lone parent benefits, even though her company hadn't made a penny.

Eventually, despite securing a major order from Spain, Pascale threw in the towel and closed her business. She had to accept that making it a success would require far more time than she had to give. Looking back she comments: *'As well as wishing I'd had more time available, I really wish I'd had a mentor – an experienced business person to advise me on what I should do next. But in the Nineties there was a lot less help around for small businesses than there is today.'*

So was the burden of juggling being a mother and an entrepreneur really crucial to the failure of Pascale's business? Years later, with the children off her hands, she set up a very successful picture framing service (**www.stowfordframing.co.uk**) and has just launched an arts activities business, Access All Arts (**www.accessallarts.com**). This indicates to me that Pascale indeed had the ability to come up with a sound business idea – as I said in the Introduction, I believe this is typical of most people going into business – and it was indeed her personal circumstances that were the main problem. It also shows that having one start-up die on you needn't prevent you from trying again and succeeding – but only if you are willing to learn from your previous failure.

It doesn't matter what kind of business I set up, just as long as I don't have a boss anymore.

Many individuals see working for themselves as an end in itself, and cast around for any opportunity to quit the day job. While there may be nothing wrong with this attitude *per se*, it often results in people running businesses that simply aren't right for them.

For a start, as an employee, you will have got used to a certain income level and if the new business can't match that, you could soon be asking yourself why you are working longer hours for less money. Eventually, you may even decide it isn't worth the effort, close the business and return to employment, disillusioned if not a little poorer.

Just as important, you have to ask if the business is something you will enjoy doing, irrespective of the financial rewards. Setting up a shop when you hate being indoors or are uncomfortable dealing with the public, for example, is an obvious formula for failure.

The two kinds of start-up

A fundamental decision that is best made as early as possible is whether your new business will be 'lifestyle' or 'growth'?

A lifestyle business is one that will provide a relatively steady and finite income. The term comes from the idea that people choose this business option as much for the freedom and flexibility of not working for someone, as for any financial advantage it might have over being an employee. An example would be a self-employed taxi driver, whose total income is limited by the number of hours he or she can work in the day. The main advantage of a lifestyle business is limited risk.

With a growth business the money you will make is less predictable, but with no real limit in the longer term. That's because a growth business can be 'scaled up' in size to earn greater revenue. An example would be to set up a mini-cab firm which employs several drivers. Now the only limit to what you can earn is the amount of business you can attract, with more drivers employed as you get more customers; you could also open up in new locations, such as a neighbouring city. Initially, though, you will need to invest in an office, hire staff and buy radio equipment, so that you may have little or no income at the beginning, and if you don't attract enough business you could lose your initial investment.

So, if you're someone who avoids risk and wants a steady income, a working life akin to employment, but with you as the boss, a lifestyle business would be the way to go. On the other hand, if you have a genuinely entrepreneurial bent, with a desire to exploit new ideas for maximum financial benefit, and don't mind taking a risk, then a growth business is for you.

Another fundamental difference between the two types is that you are only likely to find outside investors (people willing to finance your company by buying a share of it) for the growth kind. This is because it is only with a growth business that an investor is ever likely to see a return on their capital, either from income generated above what is needed to cover salaries and running costs or from the eventual sale of the business. To emphasise the point, professional investors will always say it is only **high-growth** businesses they are interested in. Alas, there are many stories of wannabe tycoons who went looking for investment only to be told, *'Sorry mate, what you have is a lifestyle business that will only ever support yourself and provide nothing for an investor.'*

I can run a successful bar/restaurant/shop/magazine – after all, I know how to drink/eat/spend/read.

This is a Stupid Factor of the worst kind: believing there are businesses you can be successful in despite having no relevant training, no deep knowledge and absolutely no experience. This is arrogance and wilful ignorance mixed together in the perfect recipe for failure.

The thing you have to ask yourself before you start a business is: would you hire *you* for the job you are going to undertake? For example, every week people with no experience of the catering trade launch restaurants that they will both own and run. Would you expect to be hired as a restaurant manager with no experience or qualifications? Probably not, and with good reason: if you were taken on you'd effectively be training on the job, which would cost the business money. Then there's the very real possibility that you have no aptitude for restaurant work. Get the point? Just because an industry appeals to you – it's trendy or fun or just very lucrative – that doesn't mean you should leap into it. Many people do, though, and they usually justify this in retrospect by coming out with twaddle such as, *'If I knew then what I know now I probably wouldn't have started this business, so perhaps it's better that I didn't know what I was doing.'* I hope you find that statement, which I've heard many times, as annoying as I do. What it really means is that someone has wasted untold time and money (not to mention putting themselves through a living hell of incompetence and failure in the process), and now needs to justify their stupidity in some way.

'Go with what you know' may seem a dull mantra for anyone keen to be an entrepreneur, but it certainly increases your chances of success. If you stick to an industry you know well, you'll waste less time getting going and you should avoid some of the more obvious pitfalls. But if you're still keen to strike out into pastures new, there are some very simple steps you can take which will soon pay off massively in your new venture.

First off, get a job that directly relates to your new business. This could be as simple as working as a part-time waiter or waitress for a few weeks, or as a weekend shop assistant, or pulling pints at lunchtimes. For a wannabe Conran or Roddick this may seem like a ludicrous waste of time and effort, but think again. You are willing to spend perhaps over £100,000 on your enterprise but you can't spare a few hours a week for what is effectively paid training?

In addition, learn as much as you can wherever you can about the business area you're interested in. There are books that deal specifically with starting a shop, coffee bar, restaurant, etc – read one. There are innumerable vocational night classes and correspondence courses on offer – take one. There are people all around you with relevant knowledge and experience – pick their brains. All of this may seem like a lot of effort, but it's nothing compared with what you'll have to do once you're in business, and there's no doubt you'll be glad you did once you're in the thick of things.

Going into business with my friends and family will make life a lot easier.

Starting a business is a big step to take, so it's understandable that many people don't want to do it all on their own, and ask friends and family to get involved too as co-owners and managers. This isn't necessarily a bad idea: from a financial point of view it can reduce the amount of money you personally need to raise (and risk!) to get started if there are partners also putting in capital. And on a practical level there's a lot of work involved in setting up and running a business, and having others around to share the effort and responsibility can be very handy. On a more personal level, running a venture on your own can be a very lonely and stressful experience, so having people you know involved can make it a lot easier to handle.

There are, however, some less savoury aspects to setting up a business with friends and family that need to be taken into account. For a start, you may find that people you know only socially are very different animals in a work context, and you may not like what you see. It is common for best friends to quickly turn into virtual enemies under the stress and strain of running a business, when they see whole new sides to each other's personality. You therefore need to consider if you want to risk the health of your personal relationships: when they turn sour, you could soon be wishing you had gone into business either by yourself or with people you hadn't been so close to.

In fact, it is not unknown for new entrepreneurs to realise, once their venture is off the ground, that running a business isn't as difficult as they expected, and that they genuinely don't need the other people they originally got involved. This can lead to intense resentment and acrimony if the entrepreneur then tries to ditch the 'excess baggage' – boot friends and family out of the firm they helped start. You should, therefore, ask yourself what contribution your partners can actually make to your business, other than moral support and a good cup of tea. If the answer is 'not very much' then starting on your own, even if that is a little scary, may be the smarter move. (Getting friends and family involved in the ownership and running of your business is not to be confused with getting investors to put money in your business. While investors may provide help and advice, and even take a hand in some of the bigger decision making, they won't necessarily be involved in day-to-day management.)

Going into business with others

When you decide to start a business with other people you are taking a big step, whether you realise it or not. Immediately, you have to think about who owns what in the business, how the profits will be shared out and what each person's responsibilities are.

The first step should be to put any business relationship on a formal footing. See page 52 for the different kinds of business you can set up, each of which will allow you to work on a clearly defined basis with others. Whatever you do, don't work with someone on some vague notion of being 'partners' in an undefined business entity, as this can only lead to problems. After all, people have been getting together to go into business for centuries, so it's no surprise that formal legal structures, such as limited companies, have arisen to allow them to do this on a secure basis (and without the need to resort to pistols at dawn to resolve disputes). That's not to say that these guarantee there won't be any upsets between you and your colleagues, but they will certainly make life simpler if a business relationship turns sour.

Another point to consider when two or more people go into business is that you need a way of reaching decisions and acting on them. Too often when equal partners in a business discuss a plan of action, unless they all agree the next step, nothing actually gets done. Such inaction can pose a serious threat to the success of your start-up, and the simplest solution is to put someone in overall charge who is empowered to make final decisions. It is also important to make sure that an individual is responsible for each task that needs doing in the start-up. Ironically, if everyone is made responsible for everything, then no one will ever take final responsibility for anything. As you read through *Stupid Factor* you will see that many things need to be done to set up and run a successful business, so the sooner you get into the habit of allocating responsibilities amongst your associates the better.

A second important habit to adopt is to make notes at meetings. This is something that can be easily overlooked, especially with meetings between business partners. Without a summary of what has been agreed at a meeting the door is left open for disagreement in the future. A well written set of minutes, however, can act as an action plan, with a timetable for what needs doing and by whom.

Finally, business colleagues must continually communicate with each other – take time to talk about what's going on in the company. Don't simply make assumptions about how your colleagues feel about the business. And as with any relationship, don't let things fester – if you are unhappy with what your partner is or is not doing then talk to them. Keeping quiet in the hope that a strained business relationship will get better by itself rarely works.

Setting up as a consultant or freelancer is an easy, no risk way for me to start my own business. I'm good at what I do and that's all that matters.

It's not difficult to see why thousands of people in the UK see consultancy and freelancing as easy ways to go into business. They generally require little or no up-front cost, except perhaps for a new laptop. Better yet, you can generally charge an hourly rate considerably higher than what you earned as an employee – which equates to more money for less work, yippee! Furthermore, there's very little administrative effort involved – if you are going to be a sole trader all you need do is tell the tax man what you are up to within three months of starting. You will then be sent a tax reference number, put on Self Assessment and hey presto! You're running a real business. However, just because something has been easy to set up doesn't mean it will be easy to run successfully.

Most people moving into consultancy will do so because they are sure of having some initial clients, such as old employers. The challenge, though, is to continually find new business. (If you don't earn a penny for six months, it can hardly be said that setting up as a consultant hasn't cost you anything.) This may seem pretty obvious, but what isn't so obvious is that doing this will demand you get involved in activities you have no experience of. Suddenly, you have to be a marketer finding new business prospects, a salesperson turning these into paying clients, and an account manager who can keep them happy and get further business out of them. Just being good at your specialism is now no longer enough. The bottom line is that even though your consultancy only has one employee, you, it is still as much a business as Tesco or BP. Branding, budgeting, public relations, advertising, websites, marketing communications – the big boys have to worry about these things and so will you.

So it is perhaps no surprise that consultancy and freelancing for many people end up being short-term activities. Once they realise the magnitude of the effort required for ongoing success, suddenly being an employee with well defined responsibilities and regular hours doesn't seem so intolerable.

Top tips for successful consultancy and freelancing

➔ **Read the rest of this book!** One man bands are as vulnerable to Stupid Factors as any other business; they also have as much to gain by applying good business practices.

➔ **A consultant or freelancer can never have enough business contacts** – don't just rely on a small number of personal contacts to keep you going. Whether it's networking with local companies, advertising online or chatting to people at the bus stop, you must constantly work to spread the word about your consultancy. You will be amazed at the number of names you need in your prospects database to have a hope of achieving an income equivalent to what you could be earning as an employee, over the long term. You should also consider subscribing to one of the many Internet-based business networks, such as Ecadamy (www.ecadamy.com), which is a great way not only for you to seek out useful contacts, but also for others to find you. See page 56 for further discussion of networking.

➔ **Don't undersell yourself.** Your time is all you have and your supply of it is very finite (there's only 24 hours in a day), so you need to get as much for it as you can, however tempting it may be to reduce your rates to get more business. As a public relations consultant for the IT industry in the late Nineties I initially worked for £75 per day and thought that was good money. But by constantly upping my rate I eventually got to a whopping £300 per day doing exactly the same work, and I was as busy as ever.

➔ **Don't over commit yourself.** Taking on more work than you have time for means you'll soon end up a) exhausted, and b) with unhappy clients unlikely to use you again. Of course, turning down work when you are self-employed isn't easy – you never know when you are going to have a dry spell – but there is a solution. If you find yourself with too much work then that's the time to up your rates (which relates directly to the previous point about not underselling yourself). Done carefully, this should reduce the hours you work while conversely increasing your income. Saying that, I knew a freelance wedding photographer in London who was getting more leads than he could handle from his online advertising, so he doubled his rates. But what do you know, pre-marrieds now thought he was twice as good, so he got even more enquiries, which he was forced to pass on to fellow freelance snappers.

➔ **Act in a professional manner at all times.** As a solo operator you may well develop closer relationships with clients than you would as an employee in a large company – after all, when they phone your office there's only ever you to talk to. This can be an advantage for you, as clients often appreciate always being in direct contact with the person doing the actual work for them (which is not always the case when they employ larger organisations). However, that shouldn't be used as an excuse to take a more casual approach to your work. Certainly, there's no room for compromise with following through on commitments made to clients, such as achieving stated goals within agreed timeframes; politeness and courtesy at all times are also a given. The old saying that familiarity breeds contempt applies as much in the 21st century as it ever did.

➔ **Exploit the earning potential of your existing clients** as much as possible. Finding new clients can be difficult and costly; getting more work from existing clients is generally the easier and cheaper option. So if, for example, a client is a large organisation chances are it has divisions and departments you've had no contact with, but which could use your service if they knew about it. This could be done by being included on a central list of approved suppliers, by getting mentioned in internal communications such as employee newsletters, or simply by asking your existing contacts to introduce you to their colleagues.

➜ **Actively manage your clients' perception of what you are doing for them.** Often the advantage for companies of using consultants and freelancers is that they can be left to do their work with minimal supervision, unlike most employees. The disadvantage for you of this is that the client may not become aware of the skill and effort you are putting into your work for them. It is, therefore, as important to make sure they know what a great job you are doing for them as it is to actually do a great job! This can be done by scheduling regular meetings with managers, through written progress reports (even if these haven't be asked for by the client), or simply by picking up the telephone and telling them the amazing thing you've just done for them. The objective is to make sure the clients feel they are getting value for money from you, and that they have no need to look for someone else to provide the service you're giving them.

➜ **Don't let relationships go cold** once you've finished a project for a client. You can't rely on automatically being remembered the next time they need the service you provide. A regular phone call or friendly email and a card at Christmas may be all it takes to ensure they don't forget you are there. You may also want to send them regular updates on your business, for example when you relocate, introduce a new service or achieve an accreditation. Doing things like this to get business in the future is a lot easier and cheaper than hunting down brand new clients.

CASE STUDY: The MathMagician

The route to self-employment and starting your own business could be more obvious than you might think, involving something you do already, such as volunteer work, an interest or hobby, and even your existing job. In the case of 23-year-old Jessica Hawker it proved to be a combination of all these. Articulate, personable and very independently minded, she graduated with a biochemistry degree in 2004, but with no job lined up. While she investigated her various employment options and sent out the usual wad of applications, she took up science and mathematics tutoring to children as a 'stop gap'. But after talking to a number of prospective employers she realised that the job she wanted was actually the one she already had: tutoring.

Jessica had been involved in teaching special needs children, youth training and counselling even before she graduated, but had never considered teaching as a profession despite her interest in education. However, having now consciously chosen teaching as her career, Jessica quickly realised she would need help and advice to develop what she was doing on a casual basis into a proper business. This is in stark contrast to many people who decide to work freelance as, for example, copywriters, journalists, consultants, or, of course, tutors. Too often, they fail to see that what they are doing is really no different from someone who sets up a manufacturing company or buys a shop, and that they need to think about marketing and financial planning just as much as any other business person if they want long-term success.

Her first step was to see an advisor at her local Business Link who discussed with her the importance of developing a business plan, and practicalities such as managing her accounts. She then shopped around various local business support agencies to find further help, which led to her buying a 'Starting in Business' package that included a three-day course. This proved a great way to pick up useful advice, boost her own confidence, and meet other entrepreneurs in a similar position to herself – and all for just £60. She also collected a host of recommendations for useful books and websites, and even found herself a mentor. He was a high-flying international businessman who volunteered his time to meet up with Jessica every three weeks to discuss the development of her venture. This included helping her strike a balance between coming up with exciting new ideas for her business and keeping on top of the more mundane, day-to-day tasks.

The course also helped her think more creatively about something she'd already decided was important – developing an identifiable brand, rather than simply being 'Jessica Hawker: tutor'. She saw that a key part of this process was deciding what values people should associate with her business. For example, she was keen to be seen as credible and providing a valuable service. So, as an alternative to tutoring in clients' homes, she set up her own classroom, making it a safe, positive and fun learning environment clients would enjoy coming to. She added an element of style by giving her sole-trader business a snappy name, MathMagician Tuition, with the strapline 'To educate, empower and enthuse'. She also had a matching top hat logo designed to use on her business cards and website.

As her business started to take off, Jessica finally got around to writing a business plan, commenting: *'Because I fell into running my own business I didn't do it early enough. Doing a plan as early as possible helps you decide what you do and don't need to do, so that you use your time more effectively. It's important to have your main goals clearly set down and to have a timetable for achieving them.'*

Her marketing has mainly been through word of mouth: happy clients telling their friends about the great work she is doing. She also advertises in school newsletters and on notice boards in bookshops and newsagents. Jessica even incentivises her existing clients to bring in new business by offering them free tutoring sessions. She also plans to do more networking, both online and at local business events, although she currently has little trouble finding work: *'Everyone either has a child of their own or knows someone with a child that could benefit from tutoring. Word soon gets around if you're good.'*

Jessica is already looking to the future, with her business plan covering the next ten years. Goals include finding ways to turn a classic lifestyle occupation into a growth business. Jessica is investigating franchising her business, which would see her sharing her unique teaching techniques and materials with carefully chosen and suitably qualified franchisees. In fact, she has already teamed up with other tutors to provide clients with a wider range of tutoring services, under the banner Wizard Tutors (**www.wizardtutors.co.uk**). Longer term, she is even considering opening her own school. But for the moment she is focused on cultivating her core business, and gradually developing herself both as an educationalist and a businesswoman.

2

My Brilliant Idea

Some start-ups are startlingly original, providing something that's never been seen before. These often have little or no competition, but at the same time there may be no established market for what they have to offer. The people behind them can be thought of as truly entrepreneurial as they strike out into uncharted waters, taking big risks in the hope of big rewards. Other new businesses have nothing novel about them at all, and simply rely on the market being big enough to accommodate yet another company providing the same old whatever. These are often started by those who, while they may be ambitious, are certainly not looking to start any kind of revolution. It is useful to recognise early on which of these two kinds of business you are looking to start, and whether this fits in with the sort of person you are and your aspirations. Your idea for a new biz may be very clever, but is it for you?

As an example, Michael Forster, an engineering graduate in his late-twenties, set up a limited company to develop and produce smart, low-cost gadgets to make life just that little bit easier and safer for everyone. Its first product was a windscreen-mounted sticker to help car drivers drive more safely on motorways. Recognising his own shortcomings as a businessman, Michael's plan was to get marketing companies to distribute and promote this and any other products he developed, and in return they would get a big slice of the selling price. He made a successful prototype of the sticker, found a printer who could manufacture it to his specification and then met with companies willing to market his product. Things were looking good until the latter insisted that he not only be responsible for manufacturing the stickers, but also for packaging them. Suddenly, Michael was faced with what he considered a serious escalation of cost, as so far he'd got away with designing the actual sticker himself on his home computer. Hiring graphic designers, ordering plastic wrapping, physically packaging up the products, registering barcodes – he felt all this would greatly increase his financial risk, which was something he wasn't willing to do. So, alas, the safety sticker never got on the shelves and he soon had to wind up his company. Needless to say, Michael would have saved himself considerable time and money if he had realised at the beginning that his entrepreneurial business idea, though basically very sound, in no way matched his chronically risk-averse temperament. As a matter of interest, after this experience, he got hired as a computer programmer and has now been happily doing the same job for the same big corporation for over a dozen years.

But assuming you have indeed identified the right kind of start-up for you, be it entrepreneurial or otherwise, what's the next step? It is vital that you now work as hard as you can to establish reasonable grounds for thinking it can be a success. Put more plainly, you must have something more tangible than gut feeling for believing your dotcom/pizza parlour/llama farm will make a decent profit before you build the website/order the anchovies/fly to Peru.

I'm sure (or at least I hope) most of us would see this as a logical next step after having the initial idea for a business. Yet amazingly, vast numbers of people, ranging from thrill-seeking risk takers to sober pillars of the community, skip it altogether and rush lemming-like straight into physically setting up their businesses, with all the associated costs and risks. If ever you feel the urge to be a lemming, I beg you, make a cup of tea, sit down and re-read this chapter. And you should probably keep away from cliffs too.

This is such a good idea it can't fail

There's nothing like that eureka! moment when various thoughts that have been running around in your head for days suddenly fit together. Disposable razors! Wind-up radios! Bagless vacuum cleaners! Email on the move! All-you-can-eat Chinese buffets! These ideas can be so powerful and fill you with so much excitement and energy that they enable you to attain goals that previously would have been unthinkable: start a company, raise finance, lease premises, hire staff, get customers – now you can do it all.

In many respects, blinding flashes of inspiration are a good thing – they are often how people get started in business. But there is a dark side to these moments ... The fact is that people come up with great business ideas all the time, but a great idea on its own doesn't guarantee success – *there are none that are so good they can't fail.* Take video phones as an example: being able to see as well as speak to the person at the other end of a telephone line must, surely, be a great idea (as long as they don't phone when you're in the shower). However, though the technology to do this has been around since the early Seventies, only very recently, with the advent of home broadband and 3G mobile networks, has it looked remotely likely to take off commercially. In the intervening 30-odd years businesses ranging from major corporations to feisty start-ups have spent a ton of money pursuing a great concept that hasn't made anyone any profit.

So, am I saying good ideas are, erm, bad? Of course not. What I am saying is that there's something else you need to do before you even think about remortgaging your house in the belief that everyone needs a turbo-powered salad spinner. That something else, friend, is market research.

⚠ Market research costs too much money and will only waste time.

This attitude stems from a misconception about what market research is, how it's done and what it can do for you. Done properly, market research will save you both time and money. By not doing it, you will be taking unnecessary risks, miss valuable opportunities and probably blunder into very avoidable pitfalls – precisely the things that *Stupid Factor* wants you not to do.

Market research: what, why and how

It is, literally, researching the market your new business is going to be operating in by any means appropriate. What it doesn't mean, necessarily, is a middle-aged woman with a clipboard in a shopping precinct trying to get you to stand for five minutes in the rain while she asks what colour underpants you buy (or does that just happen to me?).

Before examining the ways in which you might conduct this research, we should first look at the big questions it needs to answer.

- Firstly, you want to establish the likely level of **demand** for whatever it is you want to sell – will anyone out there buy this product or service apart from your gran?

- Secondly, you want to know what **competition** you are likely to face – will you be able to grab enough market share to make a reasonable profit?

- Thirdly, you want to make sure there aren't any **other factors** that could adversely affect your business – are there any dangers you need to be aware of?

So how exactly do you get started with your research? A good way is to break each of the three big questions down into a number of specific questions that you would like answered. For example, establishing demand may mean answering the questions, **'What kind of people would want what I'm selling?'**, followed by, **'How many are there of them that I can market to?'** While you're at it, you might also want to know, **'What are they willing to pay?'** and see if this is enough to give you a profit.

When it comes to competition, you need to think in terms of direct competitors and indirect competitors. The questions are therefore typically, **'Who is selling something similar?'**, **'Do they sell to the same people I'll be chasing?'** and **'Who is providing something different, but which solves the same problems or fulfils the same needs as what I'll be selling?'**

35

Regarding 'other factors' that could prove dangerous, you will need to take a close look at the environment you will be operating in. For example, if you were opening a shop selling designer bathroom suites in a small town with a single major employer, one question would definitely be, 'Is that employer in financial difficulties and likely to lay off workers or even close down?' Or if you were starting a biotechnology company exploiting stem cell research, you would need to consider likely political and legal developments – will the government support this activity (i.e. create a positive environment) or legislate against it?

Next, you need to gather the information that will answer your questions. A lot of this may exist as facts and figures that someone has already collected and compiled, and which you can access fairly easily at little or no cost. National and local government organisations are a good place to start, as are relevant trade bodies (though these may require you to take up membership), your local Business Link or Chamber of Commerce, trade publications and market research companies (which usually charge).

Then there's market information in a more raw form, which you must collect and compile yourself. An example might be to look in Yellow Pages to see how many scooter dealers there are in a town where you want to sell scooters, what makes of scooter they sell, and what extra services they provide.

You may also need to do more basic research to answer your questions. For example, if you have found a site for a restaurant you may want to spend a day there counting the number of people walking past. Better still, you could actually ask these people specific questions about eating out – how often they do it, what they like to eat and how much they spend. The more systematic you are about doing this – asking many people the same carefully thought out questions and making an accurate note of their answers – the more useful will be the results. I once provided marketing consultancy for a telecommunications company that wanted to sell telephone systems to the emergency services.

This required an accurate picture of what telephone systems police forces and fire brigades were already using. In the end, the only way to do this was to actually phone each force and brigade in the country and talk to their telecoms officer. This was a time consuming task, but the results proved invaluable in deciding how to attack this market. But even if you take a less rigorous approach and just have general conversations with your potential customers - be they telecoms officers or potential diners – the results can still prove very useful.

A prime tool for doing much of this research is, of course, the Internet, with government websites now proving particularly good sources of information. However, it can often be quicker just to ask people who are already 'in the know'. These could be journalists (particularly on trade publications), business analysts and industry experts (often quoted in the news), business advisors (such as you find in banks and at Business Link), academics and even potential competitors (who can be surprisingly helpful if they don't perceive you as a direct threat). The key thing is to keep an open mind where the information you need could come from, and to not be afraid to pester anyone and everyone to get it.

Finally, actually use your market research. If it doesn't reveal an obvious market for your business then either conduct research or think of something else to do. You should also let your research help shape your business, perhaps by adjusting your prices or the range of services you provide. And don't be selective with the facts you use – your research should give you a complete market picture, which may include things that don't support what you want to do. In this case, be mature enough to make a balanced judgement about whether to proceed with your business idea.

I don't want to do market research because it might put me off doing what I want to do.

Done properly, yes, it may well do, but that's the point – the research should tell you if you *shouldn't* start a new business, not just why you *should* start it. As an example, a designer I knew came up with a great idea for a magazine and asked if I would invest in the project. Called *Honeymoons*, as the name suggests, its target audience was people planning their honeymoon. While there were plenty of wedding magazines already on the shelf, these didn't cover the honeymoon element to any depth and so, at first glance, it seemed that the publication would be a) unique and b) have access to a large market (many people get married every year and nearly all take a honeymoon). I was very interested in the venture and so decided to do further research. This meant establishing exactly how many people get married each year, what their magazine buying habits are (most couples buy at least two wedding magazines) and how much they spend on their honeymoons. The results of this research made the magazine seem like a definite money maker.

However, I also discovered that a few years earlier a similar publication had been launched, but had gone out of print after a few months. There could have been a multitude of reasons for this – it may have been badly produced and poorly distributed so that it never sold well enough to cover its costs; perhaps advertising sales were weaker than they should have been; or maybe its owners fell out and decided to close the magazine rather than sort out their differences (yes – that does happen with businesses!). But rather than guess, I did further research. I spoke to the agency that had been responsible for selling the advertising space, and was told that sales had gone well initially. However, when the publisher refused to provide circulation figures following the launch, and the advertisers themselves got a poor response from their advertisements, ad sales plummeted.

I then talked to the publisher himself, who proved very forthcoming. He said that sales had been very weak from the start and got worse following the tragic events of 9/11. Eventually, he concluded there was no market for a honeymoon magazine – *'People just get the information they need from the Internet or travel agent'* – and chose to close the publication.

Even after this revelation, I still wanted to continue with the project. After all, I was sure we would do a better job – *Honeymoons* would look better, contain more interesting articles, and be marketed more aggressively to both advertisers and readers. But then it struck me that I was ignoring the obvious – the previous magazine had tested the market and demonstrated it wasn't really there. We therefore abandoned the venture, despite the wealth of very positive information the market research had uncovered. It was a tough decision to make, but, given the high failure rate for new magazines, to continue with such an obvious warning sign would have been reckless. Had we simply gone with our initial enthusiasm, or chosen to be selective about our research, then we would have had all the fun of running our own magazine, but probably not much money left in our pockets.

I don't care what the research says, I'm going to do this anyway.

Now we're back to working on gut instinct and blind faith. If the research shows there's no obvious market for your business or there's too much competition or there simply isn't enough money to be made – then take heed. Unless you really don't care about throwing away lots of time, effort and money, either think of something else to do or hang on until market conditions are right for your great business idea.

If the company gets just get one per cent of the market it'll make millions!

This is the sort of thing that turns up time and again in business plans – and is usually a big turn off for potential investors. It stems from doing the market research (probably whilst wearing very rose-tinted spectacles!) but not applying any commonsense to the results. Yes, there may well be an enormous market for your new business, and yes, just a tiny fraction of it may be all you need to make a fortune, but how can you be sure of getting any share of the market? With this sort of logic the only business worth starting would be selling cola. After all, the market is vast and product margins are huge (it's only sugar water) – one per cent would make you a billionaire. But when your competitors are the likes of Coca Cola and Pepsi, getting any share of the market is likely to be a very difficult and expensive process.

What you also need to address is exactly how you will tap into the market that your research has now proved exists. To help you do this, a useful exercise is to identify a section of your overall market where you can get not just one per cent market share, but over 50 per cent. This will force you to look at your market in much finer detail and think in very practical terms about the resources required to market to the various sectors of it. Until you do something like this you won't be in a position to judge if your start-up can succeed.

⚠ Once the business is up and running, we'll soon find our customers.

You're not up and running until you get customers. Certainly, if your business will be selling a high value, low volume product or service you should have a list of customers as soon as possible. Ideally, you would want money from them before you're even trading (a deposit, say, for a limited edition sports car that's still on the drawing board) which will help cover your start-up costs. Similarly, if you're marketing a product that it is only economic to manufacture in bulk, you should look to have firm orders based on a prototype before you go into mass production.

Failing all that, you should have letters of intent or at least verbal assurances – anything that proves to you (and potential investors!) that there is a real demand for what you're doing. If you don't do this and proceed simply on general notions of a market for your business, then you could be in for a white-knuckle ride as you spend your start-up capital and then sit around waiting for customers that need never come. *'If I stock it they will buy it'* (to paraphrase from *Field of Dreams*) is not a sound basis for going into business, and indicates that you are moving too quickly from your initial idea to opening up shop. Do more research, talk to more people – don't be a lemming.

CASE STUDY: Coview

Greg Wood is a serial entrepreneur who has worked in the technology industry for 27 years. During that time he has run two start-ups that failed (his first and third – Greg is a firm believer that every good entrepreneur should have a failure or two in their past), one that was eventually sold on at a profit, and a fourth which he is currently developing and that he told me when I first met him, *'It looks like I'll be able to retire on.'* A business that proves so successful it will allow you to spend your golden years on a yacht in the Caribbean is the goal of many an entrepreneur. So when I heard that Greg might be in a position to do just that, I naturally wanted to know more. In particular, where had the big idea come from and how had he financed his venture?

Over the course of five or six years, Greg had noticed that companies, especially larger ones, were getting increasingly worried about one particular issue: ensuring all their electronic documents were up to date, and that employees weren't using 'old' information. In addition, company directors were particularly concerned that they always have accurate information on the most important aspects of their business. All of this stemmed from a combination of new legislation and pressure from regulatory authorities obliging businesses to keep documentation up to date. Also, new laws meant managers and directors could no longer plead ignorance as a defence against sub-standard or even illegal practices in their companies: they are now expected to have a clear, accurate picture of what is going on at all times.

The answer Greg came up with for all this was Coview, a system that could notify employees that documents they held on their personal computers were out of date and needed to be replaced with new versions from a central repository. It could also automatically replace those out-of-date documents if required, so that managing directors, for example, could be confident they always had the latest versions in front of them.

Turning this basic idea into a sellable software product would take more money than Greg could pull out of his own pocket. But at the same time he wasn't willing to build up massive personal debt either, having seen many fellow businessmen get into trouble that way. *'Getting the money is easy,'* he says. *'It's when you have to make the repayments that you have the problems.'*

His answer was to have his customers effectively finance the creation of his new company, Connect 360 Ltd (**www.connect360.co.uk**). Firstly, he found someone interested in using Coview to make money for themselves, and who contracted Greg to research the likely market for the product. This meant he was being paid to do something he would soon have to do anyway. He also found a company that wanted to employ the technology behind Coview in its own product, and which paid for a license allowing it to do that. This gave Connect 360 the money to actually develop that technology, as all he currently had was a very rough prototype that he himself described as 'all smoke and mirrors'.

Greg's imaginative approach to funding is becoming increasingly common amongst start-ups and is in stark contrast to the previous dotcom model. This involved getting a big wad of investment capital to launch the business, then spending like mad and not worrying too much about when you'd actually make money. Now, the founders of potentially high-growth businesses often think the other way round – getting revenue at the start to help finance the growth. This may well be born more out of necessity than choice – they would still prefer to have major investment to get started but haven't been able to find it. Even so, it shows you can get your new businesses off to a solid start without securing a huge amount of capital first. One particularly neat way of making your firm revenue earning, even before it has sold anything, is to charge prospective customers a fee to evaluate your product or service. This may, at first, sound like a sales avoidance strategy – why would anyone pay for the privilege of deciding if they want to buy from you? But it can make a lot of sense if the evaluation process will itself be of value to a customer. For example, if a security system under evaluation showed that a company's computers were open to attack by hackers, and your salespeople provided a detailed report on how this problem could be solved, then that would be something worth charging for. What new businesses should avoid is becoming unpaid consultants, providing prospects with useful information irrespective of their buying anything.

In a further example of Greg pulling his business up by its own bootstraps, he hired a very experienced technical director to handle product development without having to dish out a sky-high salary. Instead, he offered him shares in Connect 360, which not only secured him as an employee but also gave him a massive incentive to do great work.

As Greg's business began to take shape, he was also able to secure a bank loan guaranteed by the Small Firms Loan Guarantee scheme; this was followed by business angel financing from an investor who could help with the strategic management of the company. He also filed a patent, at a cost of £18,000, which he now believes was a very important move. *'Having a patent pending gave my company credibility with investors, lenders and customers,'* he says. *'It was also very useful having a search done as part of the patenting process, to see what other sorts of document management systems were already out there.'*

Four-and-a-half years after its launch, Connect 360 now has an impressive list of clients, including financial services provider Standard Life, and an impending distribution deal with British Telecom. Greg has also obtained venture capital funding to grow the marketing side of the company. So is it now time for him to pick up his golf clubs and retire? *'I wish,'* he told me, a year on from when I first spoke to him. *'There's still a lot more work that needs doing.'*

 Now that we've finally started in business, we can stop wasting time and money on market research.

You've followed the advice of *Stupid Factor* and spent time doing adequate market research to show your business idea is a potential winner. Now you've got your financing in place and started trading. Congratulations! You can forget about research and concentrate on running your company and making money, or can you?

Market research is something you should always be doing, no matter how long you've been trading. Markets evolve, competitors come and go, new technologies can change everything, and you need to keep track of these developments if you want to stay competitive. To paraphrase yet again, market research is for life, not just for starting up.

3

Start-up Stories – Shop Till You Drop

Every year, thousands of us find the idea of setting up a shop on a busy high street too seductive to resist. After all, the British love to shop, so if you're selling something they need or want, what can go wrong? Better still, leasing a small shop can be surprisingly cheap compared to the average home mortgage, so that even a modest level of sales is enough to pay the rent each month. And if it doesn't work out, all you have to do is cancel the lease, sell your remaining stock at cost, then walk away.

But hang on, if it's that easy why doesn't everyone open a shop? And why are rents so low? And what's the deal with all the charity shops that now fill up our town centres? Like it or not, retail is a tough business to be in these days, and starting up a shop, no matter how small, isn't to be done lightly. As the following case studies show, you can have two shops in the same city, catering to the same market... one fails, while the other thrives. Why?

Sycamore Children's Centre Ltd

John and Eileen Weldon, a married couple in their mid-thirties from north Bristol, wanted to set up a business that would give them 'a better lifestyle' and allow them to work for themselves. John is a computer programmer working for a medium-sized company, while Eileen has been a self-employed fitness instructor for the past 15 years.

Their first idea was to open a coffee bar, but after failing to secure a suitable site they switched their focus to setting up a shop of some kind. They found what seemed like an ideal ground floor location towards the end of a busy high street in east Bristol. This consisted of a good-sized shop front, a fairly small display area and a stockroom to the rear. The surrounding location certainly wasn't the most affluent in Bristol, but was far from poverty stricken. Crucially, the landlord was willing to take them on as tenants despite the lack of a business track record. Without much hesitation, the couple instructed their solicitor to arrange a three-year lease on the property at £6,500 a year.

But what to sell? After walking around the area and seeing what other shops had on offer, they decided to open a nursery store. Eileen comments, *'We thought people might be spending more on their kids.'* Neither she nor John had ever worked in retail, and beyond being parents themselves had no particular experience of the nursery goods business – but that didn't seem any barrier to starting their new business, Sycamore Children's Centre. It would stock children's clothing, toys and books, along with pushchairs and other baby and toddler accessories.

For financing they first went to their bank, which in principle was willing to lend £30,000 as a business loan if the Weldons agreed to put in £20,000 of their own money. However, the bank required them to write a full business plan. *'How could we do a forecast of how much we were going to spend and how much we were going to make?'* says Eileen. *'It was too much hassle, too many forms and too long to arrange, so we didn't bother with the bank and just got a loan on our house.'*

With a budget of £20,000, the Weldons spent half buying stock for the shop and the rest fitting out the premises, along with an unplanned extra £3,500 on solicitor's fees. This left nothing for developing the shop front, so they had to make do with a basic sign over the window and no canopy.

It was decided that Eileen would work full time in the shop, along with her sister as the only employee, while John kept his job until their business took off. The first week of trading went well and the couple grew very excited about the shop's future. But then sales dropped off sharply, and their lack of planning, inexperience and failure to seek any professional advice (including not even reading a small business guide before setting up) began to take its toll.

The first revelation was the cost of running the shop. Utilities, council tax, loan repayments and innumerable unpredicted expenses soon totted up to a figure twice their initial estimate. The next one was the sheer difficulty of getting people into the shop and buying merchandise – something they'd more or less taken for granted. For the first time they noticed that, while the high street as a whole was busy, the number of people actually walking past their shop wasn't all that great. Its location at the end of a run of shops, and well away from the main stores such as Woolworth and WH Smith, was suspected as not helping matters. Blame was also put on a gang of market surveyors who gathered every day between Sycamore and the central shopping precinct. Their constant attempts to stop and interrogate passers-by could easily be putting shoppers off venturing down to the shop, it was thought.

In an attempt to actively market Sycamore, the Weldons took out advertisements in the local papers, put up posters and arranged listings in the local directories. But these did little to reverse the decline in sales. They also set up an e-tail website, from which products could be ordered online. Alas, this generated just two orders a month, well short of the 50 a week needed to achieve the lower shipping rates that would make their e-commerce venture profitable.

The next step was to lower prices, although they'd always reckoned Sycamore to be better value than most other nursery stores, including the huge Mothercare towards the centre of Bristol. (Saying that, they'd never been able to compete with the superstores, including a local Asda, when it came to basics such as babies' vests.) Again, this failed to boost sales, leaving the Weldons very short on an answer to their increasingly dire financial predicament. They were struggling to take more than £350 a week at the till – massively short of the £175 a day that would be needed to break even.

Eventually, after ten months, the couple were forced to have a below-cost clearance sale. This finally brought in the extra customers they'd been desperately searching for, but it was too late. As their funds finally dried up, they were forced to close down the shop.

Fortunately, an understanding landlord let them terminate the three-year lease early, which was some compensation after losing £50,000 on their retail endeavour. To cover the debt that had built up after months of failing to make a profit, the Weldons sold their large home in desirable north Bristol and moved into a smaller dwelling close to where their shop had been. (Remember, they turned down a business loan from the bank – all the money they put in the business was in the form of personal loans.)

Summarising her experience running Sycamore, Eileen Weldon says, *'Despite everything, I did enjoy running the business. But I still don't really know why people didn't use our shop. The response to the clearance sale showed that they knew we were here, but we just didn't have the money to continue and see if the business could eventually work.*

'We certainly weren't overpriced, but perhaps people are willing to pay more for the convenience of buying toys or a pushchair at the same time they do their other shopping at the big retail parks. All I know is that whatever we put in the shop window, it still didn't get more people coming in.

'My advice to anyone else setting up a shop would be to do more research. Go around all the shopping centres in your area where there are lots of people on foot, and make sure you choose the best possible location.'

BORN

After just a few minutes talking to Eva Fernandes, it's obvious she isn't just another shopkeeper – she's a woman on a mission. Asked how BORN (**www.borndirect.com**), a stylish nursery and babycare store in a popular area a mile from Bristol city centre, came into being she immediately goes into a well practised but obviously sincere explanation. When her first child was born she was concerned about the environmental impact and cost of disposable nappies. This led her to found a campaign which educated parents about the benefits of cotton nappies – which includes actually being better for a baby's health than disposables. The success of this campaign helped her realise that while there was a demand for 'real' nappies, and products such as chemical-free toiletries and wooden toys, there was almost nowhere in Bristol to buy them off the shelf.

Eva then spent 18 months confirming to herself that there was a genuine market for what she wanted to sell. This included looking at local birth rates and obtaining figures for the growth in sales of real nappies from organisations such as The Real Nappy Campaign, Friends of the Earth and Greenpeace. The research showed there was definitely a demand for nappies by mail order, but she still couldn't be certain people would want to buy them through a shop.

Eva decided to take a calculated risk – when people see and feel these products at an ante-natal class they want to buy them, so why shouldn't they when they're demonstrated in a shop? She therefore started looking for a retail location, and found a reasonably spacious ground-floor unit on Gloucester Road requiring only minimal refurbishment. Always packed with strolling shoppers, many from the affluent middle-class neighbourhoods close by, this is one of the few high streets left in Britain that isn't dominated by chain stores and charity shops. Better still, the rent was lower than normal for this hip and happening retail strip, at a very reasonable £8,000 a year, apparently because the unit was on the slightly less popular side of the road.

The next step was to write a detailed business plan. Along with financial forecasts, this included a detailed marketing strategy which stated what would be BORN's USPs (Unique Selling Points). These were the things that would differentiate Eva's shop from competitors such as retail giants Boots and Mothercare. Top of the list was a product range that neither of these stocked, including real nappies made from unbleached cotton, top quality accessories (it was the first store in Britain to stock the Bugaboo buggy, made famous by actress mums Kate Winslet and Gwyneth Paltrow) and stylish clothing for children and mums-to-be. There was also a general commitment to supplying natural, organic and Fairtrade products, along with a determination to provide a first-rate customer service, which was perceived as lacking in the big chain stores. This was seen as important for the mature first-time parents likely to use the shop, and would require staff to have excellent product knowledge.

The venture was financed with a remortgage of the family home, as this carried lower fees than a business loan, and was co-founded by Eva with her sister Georgina, who had worked in retail management for over 20 years. The shop was given a stylish front with strong branding, and marketed at ante-natal and pregnancy yoga classes, with Eva giving short presentations. Some advertising was also tried, but it was found that word of mouth (with customers, midwives and yoga teachers recommending the shop to mums) and community networking were much more cost effective. BORN also did some PR, but while this definitely raised the profile of the store, Eva felt it did little to boost sales. An e-tail website was also established, which Eva says provides a 'nice complement' to the shop, and has since been further developed, though it has yet to bring in major revenues.

Regarding employment, a card in the shop window was found to work best. At first, BORN hired anyone suitably qualified, providing them with the necessary product and shop systems training. But Eva and Georgina soon discovered that it was vital that members of staff had a genuine empathy with the philosophy of the company – a commitment to supporting the environment and ethical trading – if they were to be effective employees. Eva also eventually found that it was important to have the shop's systems written down, so that it could function without a senior manager present. She counts not doing this as one of the company's biggest mistakes in the early days, along with some poor product choices.

BORN turned over £120,000 and made a small profit in its first year; by year two turnover was £300,000. Five years on, there are now two other BORN shops – in Bath and Stoke Newington, North London – and turnover has further increased. Expansion has been financed by selling equity to friends and family. Eva also talked to some business angels but found they had difficulty understanding the ethical nature of the business, including the fact that it wasn't all about making as much money as possible. There are also plans to grow the business through franchising and the use of sales agents, but little interest in floating on the stock market, with the associated loss of control over the ethos of the company. Yes, after five years BORN can definitely be considered a business success.

Lessons to learn

Eva's choice of business was no accident, with her passion for 'sustainable parenting' being her main motivator for setting up BORN rather than a general desire to work for herself. Also, she is working in an area – ethical nursery products, and in particular real nappies – she is very familiar with and which puts BORN in a niche market, meaning it has little direct competition. One positive consequence of this is that it isn't just reliant on parents who live close to the shop, with nearly 80 per cent of customers making a concerted effort to travel some distance to get there. BORN also has an easily identifiable market – mature, environmentally concerned parents with spending power – and has been carefully branded and marketed to appeal to these customers. There is also a body of in-house expertise, with Georgina having already worked in retail, that helped them avoid the more obvious pitfalls as they got established. Eva says they also consulted with the local Business Link, but found there was no great need for its services: *'It didn't add much.'*

In contrast, the Weldons were operating in a sector they knew little about. Indeed, the choice of a nursery store was largely arbitrary; they were enthusiastic to open a business, but selling nursery products was something of a last minute decision. This was compounded by a lack of planning and an unwillingness to seek the help they so obviously needed in setting up the business. Anyone with a reasonable knowledge of retail would surely have pointed out that a bland shop front in a questionable location, combined with a largely undistinguished product line, wasn't an obvious recipe for success. Given the money and the energy they were able to apply, the Weldons could have done much better for themselves. As is perfectly illustrated by BORN, the basic idea behind their venture definitely had the potential to be a success.

4

Laying the Foundations

Once you've established that there's a profitable market for your product, it's time to move forward – but don't splash out on your designer desk lamps yet! This is still a preparation phase, with no major investment required. It culminates in the creation of your business plan – the scary-sounding document you've undoubtedly heard rumours about, and probably think will be as much fun to write as having a double root canal without anaesthetic. But don't panic, *Stupid Factor* comes with Novocaine included.

⚠ There's no time to lose – I need to get started NOW!

There are two aspects to this Stupid Factor. Firstly, you should never rush into any business without adequate preparation. It's easy to think that every week that goes by without being in business is a lost opportunity to make money. But even just a little planning can increase your profitability and significantly reduce your risk. So, in the same way that you shouldn't skip doing adequate market research, don't give yourself too little time to plan and prepare.

The second point is that for any business there will be an optimal time to enter the market, which could depend on the time of year, the state of the economy or some other factor beyond your immediate control (see the e-go systems story, page 110, for an example of a start-up which was wholly dependent on the timing of developments to the national telecommunications infrastructure). If you get started too early, you might run out of money and go bust before the perfect time for your business arrives. Of course, leaving it too late is risky as well. With a shop, you may miss the optimal time for selling, or for a more entrepreneurial venture, competitors could suddenly appear and dominate an emerging market before you get started. The point is that the timing for your start-up should be dependent on business considerations, not your impatience (too soon) or inertia (too late).

What sort of business should it be?

There are four basic options for your new business: sole trader, partnership, limited liability partnership (LLP) and limited company (Ltd or plc). The best choice will depend on your individual circumstances, what your business will be about, who else will be involved in running it, how it will be financed and how you envisage the business developing. A good starting point for making your decision is to talk to your solicitor or accountant. He or she can say which will be the most tax efficient for you or minimises your personal risk or is most appropriate if you plan to raise outside investment.

Sole trader

This is as simple as it gets - working for yourself with no partners. Apart from telling HM Revenue & Customs what you're doing within three months of commencing trading, there's nothing else you need to do to get started. There are no registration fees or complicated forms to fill in, and the money your business makes will simply be taxed as your personal income. The principle disadvantage of being a sole trader is that you will be personally liable for the debts of your business. So if your business runs out of money and stops trading, you will still be responsible for paying off any creditors.

Partnership

This is you plus one or more others running a business together. Unlike a limited company, a partnership is not regarded as a legal entity in its own right; in other words, the partners are the business. Thus, the partners are taxed on their share of any profit as sole traders - the partnership itself doesn't pay any tax. Also, if one partner dies, resigns or goes bankrupt, that effectively ends the partnership. This doesn't necessarily mean that you must stop trading, though.

Again, there are no registration fees or big forms to complete, and partners will be personally liable for the business's debts. When going into partnership it is important to have a solicitor draw up a written agreement between the partners about the key aspects of the business, such as how the profits are divided and what happens when the partnership is dissolved. Without such written terms there will be endless scope for disagreement in the future, which won't help anyone. Also, to put it bluntly, you will be leaving yourself wide open to getting ripped off. Greed, desperation, stress and a hundred-and-one other factors can turn even the most trustworthy friend into an opportunistic conman. Unless you have a formal agreement you will have greater difficulty getting legal redress in the event that, for example, a partner runs off with all the capital you invested in the business.

Limited Liability Partnership (LLP)

This is similar to a normal partnership except that, as the name implies, partners – who could be individuals or limited companies – enjoy limited liability. This means if things go wrong your losses will be limited to any money you invested in the LLP plus any personally guaranteed loans.

The luxury of limited liability doesn't come without some effort: the LLP must be registered with Companies House and also file accounts and an annual return there. (Companies House is an agency that is part of the Department of Trade and Industry. It keeps a central registry of limited liability businesses which is made open to the public through its website, **www.companies house.co.uk**.) In addition, when setting up an LLP, there must be two 'designated members', who have greater legal responsibilities regarding the partnership. Individual partners and the LLP itself must all make self-assessment tax returns; individuals pay income tax and national insurance on their share

→ → →

of any profits, limited companies that are partners pay corporation tax. Once again, a written agreement between partners is highly recommended.

Limited company

These are legal entities in their own right, with finances that are clearly distinct from their owners. They can be owned by one or more people, or other limited companies, all of whom will hold shares in the company. 'Limited' means that the shareholders and directors have limited liability, i.e. they are not personally liable for the debts of the company. However, any money they have invested in or lent to the company may be lost if the business fails. Limited companies must be registered with Companies House (for a fee) and file accounts and an annual return there; Companies House must also be notified of any change of directors. The shares of a private limited company (Ltd) cannot be offered to the public, such as through a stock exchange; with a public limited company (plc) they can be. An Ltd must have at least one director and a company secretary; a plc needs at least two directors, a company secretary and to have issued £50,000+ worth of shares.

Limited companies are ideal if you are looking to raise capital from investors for a growth business – you simply hand over shares in return for their money. They can also be useful for lifestyle businesses, but in this case you should take advice from your accountant first. Starting a limited company is fairly straightforward – talk to your solicitor or a specialist supplier of off-the-shelf companies, which come either with an existing name or one of your choosing. A limited company need not trade under the official name registered at Companies House.

Limited liability is a big benefit of choosing this kind of business; the downside is greater complication and added legal responsibilities. What's more, suppliers will be only too aware that you have limited liability, and so may demand that you and the other directors personally guarantee to pay their invoices – in effect, waiving your limited liability. Think very carefully before you agree to do this.

There's no point getting anyone's opinion on my business idea, so I'll just keep it to myself.

Would-be entrepreneurs can be surprisingly reluctant to talk about their ideas, and not just because they don't want anyone to steal them. It can also result from a fear that people might not view them in as positive a light as they do, with any critical questioning taken as a personal affront. But be realistic: when you start trading, the whole world will know about your business, so you should be able to talk to someone about it now. Not least, the very act of explaining your big idea will force you to think in concrete terms about what it is your business will actually be doing. If people find this difficult to understand, then chances are you still don't really know what your business will be about. Talking to people can, therefore, be a perfect opportunity to define your business – what it will be selling and how it will actually make money. In the late Nineties, many soon-to-go-bust dotcoms would have benefited enormously from doing this.

Having decided that you will tell people what you've been up to, locked in your back bedroom on the Internet for the past month (when you've been doing your market research, of course), the next question is who to tell? The main thing here is not to only tell friends and family, who will feel obliged to say positive things about what you are doing. You also need to talk to a few cynics who aren't afraid to provide an honest opinion. In fact, you should actively seek out negative comments from people who can see potential problems – that will make you think even harder about whether your business idea is a goer or not.

I don't need any help, I know what I'm doing.

Do you really know? If you haven't started up a company before, then chances are you don't, even if you have got an MBA from Henley or a PhD from the University of Life and A-levels from the School of Hard Knocks. From the start, like it or not, you are going to need help, advice and wise counsel if you are going to succeed. What you can't rely on is miraculously knowing what to do, and dodging pitfalls despite your lack of experience. This would be the equivalent of walking into a casino and betting all the money you have on a game you don't know the rules to – you could win, but the odds are very much against you.

How to get help and advice

The key thing is to not work in isolation, and to make as much use as possible of the plentiful help and advice that's out there – much of which will be free for goodness sake!

So where do you find all this wisdom? Your first port of call could be friends and family – does someone close to you have experience of going into business? Even if you're launching a cutting edge, hi-tech company, and the only person you can think of is your cousin who opened a poodle parlour, don't let pride get in the way of talking over your business idea with him or her.

Then there are the various professionals you'll be obliged to get involved with – your bank manager, accountant and solicitor. If these are chosen carefully (see Chapter 8) they should prove an invaluable source of advice – after all, they'll have seen many people doing what you are about to do. They'll know the types of mistakes that get made, and also what the smart moves are that save time and money.

There's also a wealth of government-supported organisations, on both a local and national level, that can provide help and information. Top of the list is your local Business Link which will have business advisors who are paid to provide help to businesses in all stages of development. They also organise short courses specifically for those wanting to set up in business for the first time. At the very least, you should visit your local Link website which will be packed with up-to-date business information and advice. In addition, Business Link can hook you up with mentors and coaches who can help at all stages in the planning, development and growth of your business (see page 73).

Academic institutions also provide a lot of help for start-ups. This could be a local business school or university with an outreach programme intended to support local businesses. These often provide advice in the form of short courses, seminar programmes, research projects (with your new business being one of the guinea pigs) and speaker evenings, all of which may   Networking is another great way to avoid becoming isolated as one of the guinea pigs) and speaker evenings, all of which may cost you little or nothing and provide excellent opportunities to network...

Networking is another great way to avoid becoming isolated as you beaver away on your project. It's all about meeting people in your local business community (or, on a national level, in your business sector) to exchange ideas, pick up tips, spread gossip and even, possibly, do business with each other. This could be done simply by hanging out at the right bars and buying anyone in a dark suit or pleated skirt a drink, but there are slightly more systematic (and less cirrhotic) methods. There are online business networks where you can find and communicate with people and companies (and others can find and contact you) by searching membership databases. Also, your local chamber of commerce or Business Link will hold regular networking events that will give you a chance to talk to local business people, some of whom could be potential customers or suppliers. And business associations, which may be specific to a location or a business sector, often organise events which, while they may not be specifically intended for networking, can still be a great place to meet useful people, as long as you are willing shake hands and chat to people (mother was wrong – you should talk to strangers). Indeed, starting a business is the perfect time to shake off any residual adolescent shyness. Working a room – circulating around, talking to as many people as possible and exchanging business cards – should become second nature to all budding Bransons.

Then there are the increasing numbers of regular lunches, dinners and 'gatherings' put together by event companies precisely to fulfil the current demand for networking opportunities. These activities come at a price (with the organisers, reasonably enough, looking to make a profit) and so some discretion should be shown in choosing which to attend. For example, if finding investors is your top priority, then lunch with local business services providers (printers, advertising agencies, solicitors, etc) may not be worth the expense. However, an evening seminar where entrepreneurs make presentations to potential investors (such as takes place, in the technology sector, at First Tuesday events, **www.firsttuesday .com**) could be perfect.

The sooner you look for help and advice when planning and setting up your new business the greater will be your chances of success.

Prof Birchall says:

Networking is increasingly important for all managers, but especially those in new businesses. How are your networking skills? We all like to think we are good at relating to people, and can therefore network. But the individuals who are really good at networking are all the time fostering and developing their network, so that they can use it more effectively. Hand in hand with their business aspirations, they are always trying to move it up a notch, from perhaps being a local gathering of like-minded individuals to something involving 'higher level' groups. Also, along with PR and other promotional activities, networking can be a great way for start-ups to get involved with the big corporates. Many entrepreneurs are too absorbed in everyday problem solving to see the bigger issues and therefore develop their businesses; networking with challenging people is one way for them to move beyond the day-to-day and see how they can take their businesses forward.

 I'm the only senior manager that my growth business will need, so I've no need to waste money on expensive staff.

It's tempting to see yourself as the only high-powered employee your company will require. After all, you came up with the idea for the business, and your expected profits will be much higher if you only employ teenagers on the minimum wage. But think again – do you really have all the necessary expertise to make the business a success? Are you any good at managing employees? Do you know how to organise and motivate a sales team? Can you get your head round company finances? Can you come up with even more good ideas to ensure your start-up remains competitive as it begins to expand?

The point here is that you can deal with any weaknesses in yourself by gathering people around you who have the qualities you lack – don't pretend you can perform any and all senior management functions when you can't. This could even mean not taking the top job in the company. For example, in your new technology company you might take the role of technical director and hire someone else to be the managing director, because you have the focus and the vision, but you aren't a leader.

And if you're setting up a high-growth business, then as early as possible you must think about the management team that will run it. Some surprisingly large enterprises can be run with just a single senior manager – namely its founder. But this lack of senior talent can soon become a limiting factor, so that a high-growth business ends up being more like a lifestyle one.

Another reason for having a team in place sooner rather than later is finance. Investors will be more interested in a company with strong management already in place (or at least in the process of being recruited) than one dependent on the energy and abilities of an individual. In fact, the calibre of the management team – sales and service directors, financial director, head of product development, etc – is always a pivotal factor when venture capitalists decide whether to invest in a high-growth business. And the managers of some business angel networks strongly advise against their members ever investing in a lone entrepreneur – *'We never see good results from that situation,'* as one told me.

Location, location, location

Where you actually set up your business is something you should consider fairly early on in your planning. This can be broken down into geography (where in the country) and the immediate environment that will best suit your business. The former will depend on a number of factors, including: where you live now (you may not want to relocate away from family, friends and local contacts); where your customers and suppliers are; transportation links (would it be useful to be near an international airport or have easy access to the motorway network?); communications facilities (if you need a broadband Internet connection this may not be possible in a rural setting); cost (rent and property prices vary around the country, and also between urban and rural locations); and availability of a suitably skilled workforce. Another big consideration may be the availability of grants. For example, many business people in the relatively affluent Bristol-Bath region choose to set up their companies just over the border in South Wales where government-backed funding for start-ups is more readily available (see Grants, page 110).

Choose your space

Just as important is deciding the type of place you want to be located in. Working from your spare bedroom or your garage (as long as the council doesn't object) may be an ideal solution for a one-man enterprise looking to keep costs down. Then again, having a formal office or a shop front (which can be useful for attracting customers even if you aren't a retail business) may be important.

For an office, you might consider using serviced facilities in a business centre. These are usually more expensive than space-only renting, but you don't have the hassle and added cost of refurbishment, organising telephones, installing a computer network or buying furniture. They can also give your business a more professional appearance, with a staffed reception area and a shared telephonist to receive calls. Serviced offices can also come with very flexible leasing arrangements, including minimal notice periods. This can be very useful if you aren't sure how your business will develop – for example, how many employees you will eventually take on or even your final geographical location. Being tied down to unsuitable rented or purchased accommodation can quickly prove a false economy.

Then there are centres specifically intended to help start-ups, which are often subsidised by local councils or government-funded organisations. These can include units for light industrial use as well as offices. And for high-growth technology companies, incubators are a popular choice.

Incubators

These are generally associated with academic institutions, often include laboratory facilities and can be an ideal first location for a hi-tech, high-growth start-up. Some even provide space for entrepreneurs who are still at the very earliest stages of planning their new business. In fact, they are so attractive – not least because they are often heavily subsidised – that there is considerable competition to get into them, with strict criteria applied to determine a company's suitability.

In many ways, an incubator can be heaven for a start-up, with everything you need to avoid Stupid Factors. Along with the more obvious business facilities, they include in-house advisors who are there specifically to help your start-up develop. They will do this both informally and through regular reviews. (One disadvantage of this is that if it's decided your company is turning out to be a lifestyle business you will be asked to leave.) They are also ideal places to network, both with other entrepreneurs and the wider technical and business communities – chances are you'll find a mentor there or even your first non-executive director or chairman (these are basically professional advisors, without day-to-day operational responsibilities within the company who are usually employed part-time). Being in an incubator can even enhance your credibility with potential lenders and investors.

Other location considerations

If you are setting up a shop or restaurant then you must do as much research as you can into a possible site. This includes looking at the population in your catchment area (does the town have enough people of the right age or income group or with appropriate lifestyle aspirations for what you're selling?); your general location (will being in a prestige out-of-town shopping mall generate enough extra income to justify the high rent?); and the 'micro-environment' of the specific property (being at the slow end of even the busiest high street can spell disaster if you don't get enough punters strolling past).

For a creative business, such as a design agency, you might benefit from being in a stimulating environment (in terms of the office itself and its general location) to attract and retain the best staff, and to get the most out of them. Doing good work and coming up with great ideas when you're in a cramped, grotty office on muggers' mile is never easy, as I can testify from experience. (I've also observed that even a swish office suite with original artwork on the walls and its own coffee bar can't compensate for bad management that has left employees poorly motivated.)

 ### I don't need to write a business plan.

Yes you do! But before I explain exactly why, I'll look at some stupid reasons I've come across for people not doing so.

'A business plan is just something to show potential investors or lenders, such as a bank.' Therefore, if you are financing the business yourself, perhaps by remortgaging your home, there's no need to write one. Wrong! The fact that the plan is just for your benefit makes it no less important.

'I've done business plans before and they didn't prove useful.' If that's the case either you weren't writing an effective plan or you weren't using it properly. A well written plan will definitely help when you start your business.

'My company needs to be as flexible as possible, so I don't want to

be tied down to a plan.' This kind of thinking can arise when people go into business without a clear idea of what it is they ultimately want to do, which is something that happens surprisingly often. The trouble with this 'accidental' approach to business is that before you know it, you're expending a lot of effort and spending wads of cash without a proper appreciation of your risks and returns. You should consider delaying trading till you can write a meaningful plan, otherwise start composing one as soon as you have any inkling of the final direction your business will take.

'It sounds like hard work, so I can't be bothered.' A well written plan should be hard work, but this will be nothing compared to when you are running your new company. If you don't want to put the effort in now, then think twice about whether you're really up to the challenge of starting a business.

Your business plan: what, why and how

A basic business plan is simply a written down version of what you have probably been telling friends and relative for ages: how you have this great idea for a business and why you think it will be a success. The reason you should bother writing this down is because there is a big difference between thinking something or even telling someone something, and putting it on paper. Only in the latter case can you or anyone else really tell if it makes sense or not. Plus, the very act of writing it will force you to think more clearly about what it is you want to do.

It's possible to produce an adequate-looking business plan in a few hours, but your objective shouldn't be to write it as quickly as possible. As you go through the process of creating the plan, questions will inevitably arise that you won't be able to answer immediately. Perhaps you will see that international marketing will be important, but you have no idea how this is done or what it will cost. You should, therefore, take the time to learn about this subject so that you can put something detailed and meaningful about it in the plan, rather than skimming over it. This means the plan will take much longer to write, but the very

→ → →

---

process of creating it will prepare you for the challenges that lie ahead.

Putting together the business plan is also your chance to identify the key things that need to happen for your start-up to get off the ground. For example, if your business will be to hire out a luxury yacht in the Mediterranean, you should determine what local regulations will apply and which official permits you will need. You then need to find out what the procedure is for getting those permits and how long this takes. Just assuming that it will take a few days then discovering, after you have bought the yacht and hired the crew, that it will take six months, and you can't sail until you have them, could put your whole business in jeopardy. Creating the plan can help you spot the trip wires peculiar to your particular business.

It will also let you see what things need to be done in parallel rather than sequentially. All too often, start-ups get into trouble by thinking in terms of doing one thing at a time, and not moving on to the next task until the current task is completed, which results in avoidable delays and extra costs. But with a detailed business plan in your hands you can be more like a master chef, preparing all the elements of a great meal so that they come together at exactly the right time. Coming back to the yacht hire business, you might plan to make your permit applications one of the first things you do given the six-month delay, and schedule other activities, such as finding a mooring or setting up a website, to be done while these are being processed.

So what exactly should be in your business plan? Firstly, a **description of the business** that clearly shows how it will work and make money – also known as the business model. To get you used to thinking in terms of models, imagine what might have been in the original business plan of other companies. The business model for lastminute.com could have been along the lines of *'selling holidays and airline tickets which are about to expire at discounted prices through a website'*. Being able to summarise what it is your start-up will be doing in a paragraph or even a single sentence is very useful. Not only will it help

➔ ➔ ➔

investors and customers understand what you do, it indicates that you have a very clear picture of what you're about. You should also state what your objectives are for the business, other than 'to make lots of money'. This could be in the form of a mission statement – *'To be the biggest supplier of the best widgets in the UK'* – or be put in strictly financial terms – *'In five years to own half the market for widgets in the UK with a turnover of over £50million'*. Doing this will help you keep your efforts focused as your firm develops and grows.

There must also be a **marketing plan** which clearly states who your customers are and how you access them. This is a great chance to use the facts and figures your market research will have thrown up, as it's important to have plenty of detail here. For example, you might include the rate at which your market is growing or the likely effects of any new legislation. Distribution and pricing policy should be included along with an explanation of your USPs – Unique Selling Points. These are the things that differentiate your business from your direct and indirect competitors. It could be a unique way of selling something that they also sell, or a product only you have which has useful features the competition's offerings don't have. If you can't think of any USPs then this is a warning signal, as all successful businesses have them and those that don't usually struggle.

A **timetable** is important, stating what needs to be done and when. This is where you can include a lot of the detail of how you will set up your business. And there should be a **description of yourself and the rest of your management team**, indicating each person's strengths and who will be responsible for what. You can also put down what key positions will need filling, as well as your general workforce requirements, recruitment strategy and your approach to managing staff.

At the heart of your business plan should be your **financial plan**. This will explain how much money you need to get started, how you will get it and your revenue projections – how much money you expect to make. See **Financial Planning**, page 69, for further advice. → → →

A business plan written simply for use by yourself and your colleagues can have whatever format you think appropriate. But if you will be showing your plan to potential lenders and investors, there are some basic rules you should follow. Most importantly, the first page needs to be a powerful executive summary that grabs the reader's attention and encourages him or her to read the rest of the plan. Along with explaining your business model as clearly and succinctly as possible, you should also highlight what's hot and exciting about it, such as a new piece of technology or an original marketing strategy. In addition, there must be a financial summary that includes the lending or investment required, the estimated return on any investment, plus projected annual sales and profit for the first five years. Your plan should be just 20 pages or so long, not including appendices (documentation you might want to put in to back up any assertions you make), so leave out the nitty-gritty details that investors don't really need to know.

Each lender and investor may have a standard format they prefer for the business plans they look at, so you might want to consult with them before sending anything. For a suggested layout refer to Appendix 1 and also see **Outside investment: getting your foot in the door**, page 93, for further suggestions on what to include in the plan if you are approaching investors.

Lastly, don't be afraid to get help putting together your business plan, possibly from an accountant, the business advisor at your bank or the local Business Link. But make sure it's you who actually writes the document – trust me, you'll enjoy doing it.

Prof Birchall says:

Planning is as important for start-ups and smaller businesses as it is for an international corporation. It's all about seeing how you will keep moving your business forward, rather than getting stuck in the rut of just 'doing' (i.e. spending all your time handling the day-to-day issues that won't contribute towards your business developing in the longer term). Indeed, one reason why many new firms are not successful is because the founders' initial good idea hasn't been worked through well enough to see how, exactly, the associated product or service can be taken to market.

They also haven't thought enough about how they can protect their offering from being copied and sold by others. If you can't protect what you sell then there is sure to be someone who can provide it more cheaply than you. This is principally done through the assertion of Intellectual Property rights (see **Getting a patent costs a fortune and isn't worth the hassle**, page 122). But if that isn't possible (as is often the case with service-based businesses), you will have to think of other ways of staying ahead of the competition, as they turn your initial brilliant idea into just another commodity item. The key to this is having a constant flow of creative ideas which leads to continual improvement. You'll also need to be able to learn faster than the competition, so that you're always one step ahead when it comes to developments in the marketplace or technological innovations. And if you are, indeed, able to stay ahead of the rest, the reward should be an ongoing demand from your customers for your newest offerings. These and many other strategic issues need to be part of your plan for the business.

A particular issue faced by businesses in the hi-tech sector is that most innovations are not based on one single piece of technology, but require a combination of technologies. But small hi-tech companies usually only have the 'one piece' to contribute towards the final big idea, which will be marketed by the Sonys, IBMs and Ericssons of this world. They therefore need to take account of this in their planning by, for example, considering who their strategic partners will be and what are the compatible technologies. ➔➔➔

> In the case of service-based businesses, their principle challenge is getting customers to appreciate what they are offering them – because a service is something they can't necessarily see or touch. What the entrepreneurs are often selling is the ability to solve customers' problems in a creative way; to bring new ideas; and to deliver on time what they said they are going to deliver. Understanding what you want and having a philosophy of how you will achieve this is key to making a business like this work – so make your values and principles the starting point for your planning.
>
> Self-awareness and self-understanding are also important for success in business and shouldn't be left out of the planning process. Will you use coaching, mentoring, action learning or some other technique to help develop this side of yourself in business? (See **Coaching, mentoring and more**, page 73.)

 There's no point spending time on financial planning, as it's impossible to predict how things will turn out in real life. Anyway, I'm not an accountant, I wouldn't know where to begin.

Business is all about the numbers, and don't let anyone tell you otherwise. Okay, so you're keen to experience the personal satisfaction to be had from being your own boss. Or maybe you're motivated by ethics, and getting the world turned on to organic Fairtrade mung beans is important to you for spiritual reasons. In either case, the critical thing is still the numbers; if you don't make enough profit, or you suddenly find your company is cash embarrassed because money is going out faster than it's coming in, then everything else soon becomes irrelevant. So the bad news is there's no getting away from the numbers, even if numbers aren't your forte. The good news is that numbers don't have to be scary, and you certainly don't have to be an accountant to put together the figures you need to plan your business.

In fact, it might reassure you to be told that it's unrealistic to expect your financial prophesising to be pinpoint accurate. Ask anyone who looks at financial plans for a living, such as a venture capitalist, and they'll tell you that they're often well off the mark when it comes to predicting growth and profit. (But then that's probably no surprise, as anyone looking for outside investment is bound to inflate these aspects.) However, they should definitely indicate the viability of a business (i.e. tell you if it's capable of making money or not).

This is because there are many elements of a financial plan which can be very accurately determined. For example, costs, both start-up and on-going, can be assessed very precisely for many enterprises (but only if you put in the research effort!). Likewise, you should be able to determine a minimum and a maximum for your turnover (i.e. the total amount of money you will take off customers) without being an accountant. If maximum possible turnover is less than your ongoing costs and a proportion of your start-up costs (such as the repayments on any loans), then you will see immediately that your business can't make a profit.

Imagine we plan to open a restaurant that can seat 25 diners in a village where no one is likely to pay more than £20 for an evening meal and £5 for lunch (something our market research has told us). We can immediately see that our maximum possible turnover per week, assuming a single sitting for lunch and dinner, and with the place chockablock day and night, is £4,375 (25x20x7+25x5x7). Our research tells us that after variable costs (ingredients, staff wages, etc.) our gross profit would be half of turnover, £2,187. Not bad, you may say, but what about the fixed costs (overheads)? After totting up items such as mortgage repayments, rates and repayments on a big loan used to decorate and furnish the premises these come to £2,000 a week, leaving a weekly net profit of just £187 per week. It is now immediately obvious that our little eatery is not worth the risk – just one slow night a week would see us making a loss. If we are still determined to get into the restaurant business we need to either find a location that seats more diners or reduce our fixed costs – perhaps by renting instead of buying the property, or not spending so much on refurbishment. So you see, the numbers are important.

Financial planning, in the form of a cashflow forecast, should also predict with accuracy when extra money will be needed, beyond your bare minimum start-up costs. For many new businesses, these 'pressure points' may arise irrespective of how successful they are initially and must be anticipated. This would be the case for a magazine which has to meet its print costs well before it gets any money from newsstand sales and advertising. In fact, poor cashflow (often in the form of overtrading, see page 135), rather than lack of customers, is the number one killer of smaller UK businesses, so this is not a part of your planning to be glossed over.

Financial planning

A reasonably detailed financial plan should be an integral part of your business plan. It should provide revenue projections and profit forecasts for at least three years in advance, as well as a full costing of the start-up capital you will need and any further financing that will be required to achieve your business objectives. Here you will explain in detail how much money you need from a lender or investor and what it will be used for.

Creating a financial plan may seem a daunting task, but if you approach it in stages it shouldn't prove too difficult. The best way to do it is using a computer with either a spreadsheet or financial program, some of which are developed specifically for creating a business plan. This will allow you to constantly amend your financial plan as you get more information and also to quickly test different scenarios, with different levels of costs or revenues. You might start by looking at all the costs involved in starting your business, such as conducting market research and buying computers, which will give a first indication of how much capital you will need. Err on the side of caution and take a pessimistic view with these costs - expenses are guaranteed to crop up that weren't included in your plans. Next, look at the month-by-month cost of running the business – include fixed overheads such as utilities and salaries, as well as manufacturing costs, marketing budget, loan repayments, everything. Then compare this to your expected monthly revenues to work out your monthly profit (or loss, if it will take you some time to get to a healthy level of sales).

You must also analyse your cashflow - the total sum of money entering or leaving the business – by estimating when you will have to pay suppliers and when you are likely to get the money you are owed from customers. This could prove a very interesting moment in your planning, as you see that money will be leaving your business for months after its launch with very little coming in, even if sales are good. This, in turn, will show you that you may need more start-up capital than what is required simply to cover initial costs. It's also worth playing around with the figures, such as seeing the minimum revenue you will require to break even or observing what happens if costs prove twice as high as your original estimate or you get better payment terms from suppliers. This will give you an idea of how risky your venture is – if you can only make a profit with very strong sales then you'll need to think hard about how likely that is to happen.

Overleaf is a spreadsheet showing a simple cashflow forecast for the quarterly magazine, *Honeymoons* (see **I don't want to do market research because it might put me off doing what I want to do**, page 37). This assumes start-up capital of £60,000, and that payment terms can be negotiated with the printers so that their invoices are each paid in three instalments. Note that in November 2006 the business will have a serious cash crisis unless more capital is found. This results from the expected delay in actually receiving advertising and retail sales revenues.

Month	May-06	June	July	Aug	Sept	Oct	Nov	Dec	Jan-07
Publishing schedule					issue 1			issue 2	
OUTGOINGS									
Salaries		-3300	-3300	-3300	-3300	-3300	-3300	-3300	-3300
Misc. costs		-1400	-400	-400	-600	-600	-600	-600	
Editorial costs						-5000			-5000
Marketing costs		-500	-500	-3500	-3500	-2000	-2000	-2000	-2000
Retailer fees				-10000			-5000		
Ad sales commission						-4000	-4000		-4000
Reprographic costs						-1500			-1500
Print costs					-20000	-20000	-20000	-20000	-20000
Computer purchases		-3000							
Office rent, rates, utilities		-400	-400	-400	-400	-400	-400	-400	-400
CASH RECEIVED									
Advertising revenue						27000	27000	27000	27000
Retail sales revenue								56000	
Monthly cashflow	0	-8600	-4600	-17600	-27800	-9800	-8300	56700	-9800
Running cashflow	0	-8600	-13200	-30800	-58600	-68400	-76700	-20000	-29800
Current account	60000	51400	46800	29200	1400	-8400	-16700	40000	30200

	Feb	March	April	May	June	July	Aug	Sept	Oct	Nov	Dec
		issue 3			issue 4			issue 5			issue 6
	-3300	-3300	-3300	-3300	-3300	-3300	-3300	-3300	-3300	-3300	-3300
	-600	-600	-600	-600	-600	-600	-600	-600	-600	-600	-600
			-5000			-5000			-5000		
	-2000	-2000	-2000	-2000	-2000	-2000	-2000	-2000	-2000	-2000	-2000
	-5000										
	-4000		-4000	-4000		-4000	-4000		-4000	-4000	
		-1500			-1500				-1500		-1500
	-20000	-20000	-20000	-20000	-20000	-20000	-20000	-20000	-20000	-20000	-20000
	-400	-400	-400	-400	-400	-400	-400	-400	-400	-300	-300
	27000	27000	27000	27000	27000	27000	27000	27000	27000	27000	27000
		56000			56000			56000			56000
	-8300	56700	-9800	-3300	56700	-9800	-3300	56700	-9800	-3200	55300
	-38100	18600	8800	5500	62200	52400	49100	105800	96000	92800	148100
	21900	78600	68800	65500	122200	112400	109100	165800	156000	152800	208100

My plans will simply have to fit in with the money I have available.

Starting a new business will cost what it's going to cost, however much you'd like it to match the money you have to hand. One effect of this Stupid Factor is that business plans are tweaked until they magically produce a figure that matches what you happen to have in the bank. This is done by taking a very unrealistic view of costs, an over-optimistic assessment of cashflow (e.g. customers always pay you on time and suppliers always give you very generous payment terms) or by allocating inadequate resources to a 'peripheral' business activity. In the latter case, this could mean having little or no marketing budget, or having a plain shop front, or under-designed branding and packaging, or no dedicated after-sales support. These are all things that can seem like luxuries when you are absorbed in setting up your business, but which become vital once you're trying to get and keep customers – which is what your business is really all about.

In short, don't let the money you have easy access to dictate your budget. If you need more money to get the business started properly then find it (see the Chapter 8, **High Finance**, to find out how), or you're risking early failure. Even if you are able to scrape by with your limited start-up capital, you will generally be making life unnecessarily hard for yourself – your business will grow much more slowly as a result, so that it ends up having been a false economy. This would be the case were you to trim your budget for opening a hotel by taking on too few staff and allocating too much of the workload to yourself. You'd then spend most of your days dashing around cleaning rooms and cooking food, leaving no time to properly manage and market your business. The end result is that you are working long hours for not much money, when for the sake of a little extra start-up capital you could be making far more profit from your hotel and actually enjoying running it!

Coaching, mentoring and more

You wouldn't expect a world-class athlete to train for the Olympics without a coach helping them. Nor would you expect a prime minister to make all their major decisions without at least talking them over with advisors and cabinet members. So it's not unreasonable to believe you should have a similar level of guidance and support as you set up and start running your new business. And the good news is that you can, thanks to the increasing number of business coaching, mentoring and action learning programmes.

In broad terms, coaching involves a trained individual asking you questions intended to make you think hard about what you are doing. A coach need not be knowledgeable about the kind of business you are setting up, as their focus is on getting you to find your own solutions to any difficulties you may have. You may see your coach on a regular basis or find that a one-off session is all you need.

A mentor will have more specific knowledge relating to what you are doing, perhaps because he or she has started new businesses in the past or has a deep knowledge of your industry. Their approach will tend towards providing solid advice that is 100 per cent relevant to your particular situation, and you will usually have contact with him or her on a regular basis. Saying that, the distinction between a coach and a mentor is easily blurred. A mentor, for example, could act more like a coach by trying to steer you into finding your own solutions, as this will be far more beneficial to you in the long run that simply being handed the answers.

Action learning involves a trained facilitator putting you together with two or three like-minded peers from other businesses to discuss each other's problem on an equal footing. It also involves you taking a reflective approach to learning and action. This means that having consciously chosen to adopt a new approach to a particular business problem you take time to think about how effective it has been. You then consider how you might modify this approach next time the problem arises for even better results. Action learning is a great way to gain a fresh perspective on your business, and to tap into the knowledge and experience of other business people.

Prof Birchall says:

Henley Management College's action learning programmes for small and medium-sized enterprises tend to attract people who are ambitious about developing their business. The key element of action learning is the sharing of problems and experiences with people facing similar issues, and working together to find solutions. It's also a chance for business people to have their assumptions questioned, so encouraging them to be more reflective about what they are doing. Henley's action learning groups have added value for entrepreneurs because they give them access to a network of like-minded people who can provide help, give advice and share learning on key issues such as implementing change within an organisation. Action learning is something you can do at any stage in your business's development, not just at the very start.

Coaching, mentoring and action learning provide managers with someone else to talk to regarding strategy, which is especially useful when there is no-one within the business who they can turn to. By doing this they often find, to their surprise, that their challenges are very similar to the challenges faced by other small and medium-sized businesses, irrespective of what they do or the markets they serve. Finally, it is often said that managers 'don't know what they don't know', which is why these activities, along with networking, are vital for anticipating problems and dangers that you may not be immediately aware of.

5

Buying a Franchise
or an Existing Business

I'm going to ask you some questions, and I want to hear your answers loud and proud.

Do you want to run your own business and be your own boss?
YES!

Do you want to make a good living from it?
YES!

Do you have start-up capital?
YES!

Do you have energy and enthusiasm?
YES!

Are you determined to succeed?
HELL YES!

Do you have a great idea for a new business?
Erm ... sorry, no. All the best ideas seem to be taken. I suppose that means I can't go into business. Hi ho, back to the humiliation of salaried employment I go...

STOP! Even if you don't have an original idea for a start-up, or simply can't be bothered coming up with your own business model and figuring out if it will work, that needn't prevent you from running a successful business. That's because there are two other options on the table: (a) buying an existing business, and (b) purchasing a franchise. Both are perfectly respectable means of going into business and may even increase your chances of success. However, neither should be considered an easy option, and both will leave you as vulnerable to Stupid Factors as any other venture – so keep reading this book!

 Franchises are all in the food service industry. I'm not interested in hamburgers or fried chicken, so franchising isn't for me.

Not true. This area was an early exploiter of the model, but today there is a dizzying choice of franchises, ranging from print shops to beauty therapies to classic car clubs. If you can think of it, there's probably a franchise for it somewhere in the world.

 Franchises are too expensive, and all you get for your money is permission to use some big corporation's naff logo. Franchise? Nein danke.

Probably not true. They come in all shapes, sizes and prices, though if you have your heart set on buying a franchise from a well-known purveyor of fried cow it definitely won't be cheap. There's also a big variation in what you get for your money, but it should almost certainly be a lot more than just a giant, plastic M.

 Franchises are an easy way to get into business and make money because all the tough stuff is done for you.

A franchise is no easier to start and run than any other new business, requiring just as much planning, hard work and initiative to be a success. Plus, even with lots of support from a well-organised franchisor, there's still no guarantee of decent revenue.

Franchises: what they are and what you get

From your point of view (the potential franchisee), franchising is a way to exploit a successful business idea without having to go to the trouble of thinking one up yourself. For the company that came up with the business idea in the first place (the franchisor), it's a way to scale up a successful business idea without having to find new capital – effectively, they get that capital from the

---

franchisees. Sounds like a win-win situation? Often it is, but you need to have a good idea of what you're getting into before you buy a franchise, otherwise you could be in for some disappointment.

So what's the procedure for setting up a franchise? First, you need to choose the one you want. A convenient way to do this might be to visit one of the many franchise exhibitions that are held all around the country, where franchisors will be working hard to court your interest (after all, they need you as much as you might need them). You could also contact the British Franchise Association (**www.british-franchise.org**) which can provide details of its members (although not all franchisors belong); look in franchise magazines (e.g. *Franchise World* and *Business Franchise*); and keep an eye on the business-opportunities sections of newspapers. You might even try approaching a business you like the look of and simply ask if it would be willing to sell you a franchise – even if that's something it doesn't do already. But be aware, being the first franchisee will greatly increase your level of risk, as there won't be any proof that the franchise model works for this particular business. On the other hand, it should mean you can take your pick of where you set up (imagine you'd had the first McDonald's in London); you may also be able to negotiate a more favourable agreement than subsequent franchisees.

Next, you will want to get as much detail as possible on the franchise. The first thing to look at will be the franchisor's prospectus, which will give you an outline of the business and how the franchise operates. If you're still interested, you will then have a formal meeting with the franchisor. This is your chance not only to learn more about the franchise but also to get as much proof as possible to back up any assertions made in the prospectus (as ever, take nothing at face value). Following that, if you are still keen, you must talk to current and former franchisees – and not just the ones the franchisor has recommended you talk to, in case these have been groomed (or even bribed and bullied) to say nice things. You should also do

→ → →

as much independent research as you can on the franchise. At the end of all this you must have a clear picture of the following:

- the financial stability and honesty of the franchisor

- the total cost of buying the franchise (be wary of any fees not directly related to its set up and development)

- the ongoing payments you will need to make to the franchisor (the better ones will make most of their profit from this, and not from the franchise purchase price)

- what the franchisor will give you in return for all the money you're going to be giving them.

Ongoing payment is generally set up as a royalty, based on a percentage of sales (that means you will have to pay something even if you are not making a profit), or sometimes as a fixed management fee (although this arrangement gives the franchisor little incentive to support your business and help it grow). There may also be. fees relating to training and marketing. And if you are obliged to purchase stock or services from the franchisor, you must know what these will cost.

What you get back from the franchisor (other than the right to use its name and snazzy logo) should be a practical insight into its system for running a very successful business. After all, part of the reason for getting a franchise is to short-circuit the whole process of thinking up a new business and finding the best way to make it work; instead you are going straight into something that already works very well. Therefore, expect to get training on how to set up, run and market the franchise (yes, you will have to market and sell like any other start-up – you can't just rely on the marketing that the franchisor does centrally). There should also be plenty of ongoing support such as advice on suitable premises and equipment, temporary cover for when you take a holiday, a help line for day-to-day issues and the sharing of market research. The franchisor may also provide some important items, for example insurance, at a discount by buying centrally on behalf of all the franchisees.

As you're doing all this researching and assessing and checking, it is vital you always view your prospective franchise as a start-up, and not as a new branch of an established business. That means doing all the things any other entrepreneur has to do, such as your own market research and choosing an optimal location for your venture (and if it's clear all the best territories have been taken by other franchisees, think twice about accepting second best). Most importantly, you must write your own detailed business plan which clearly demonstrates what kind of financial return you can expect and how this relates to your costs. Don't let the flattery of being accepted by a well-known franchisor blind you to the fact that what you are doing has to make business sense – if you can't clearly see how you will make a decent profit then look elsewhere.

Before finally handing over any money (including non-refundable deposits and arrangement fees), you must get a draft agreement from the franchisor and have it checked by a solicitor who specialises in this area. This document must clearly state what you pay the franchisor, what you get in return, what obligations each has to the other, and any restrictions on how you can run your franchise (e.g. which areas you can sell in or what products you can stock). It will also say how long the franchise agreement will last (usually between five and ten years) and what happens when it is terminated. You should look for any conditions which may leave you vulnerable in the event that the franchisor proves less effective than you hoped, or sells out to a new owner with less than honourable intentions. An example of a vulnerable franchisee would be one that could only work with customers passed on to it by the franchisor.

You should be aware that franchises usually have a limited capacity for growth – almost by definition they can't be scaled up in size, because that's what the franchisor is doing by selling franchises in the first place. This fact, plus the restrictions that will be placed on how you run your business, may make this a bad choice for the more wildly ambitious entrepreneur.

CASE STUDY: A franchise horror story

In general, franchise businesses are more likely to succeed than other types of start-up. But that's not to say that a franchise doesn't carry any risk, and that you shouldn't show as much care as possible before signing contracts and handing over money. This case study isn't, thankfully, typical of what most franchisees experience, but it is a warning of what can result from making a poor choice of franchisor to work with.

George Ealing had wanted to be an entrepreneur since he was 13, when he became obsessed with the idea of becoming the next Richard Branson. At 30 it looked as if his dream might finally come true when he and his father, Donald, who had recently retired from the army, started to think seriously about setting up a parcel distribution company. George had an MA in logistical management, while Don had been an officer in the Royal Transport Corps, so between them they felt they had the potential to do well starting a business in this industry.

Through personal contacts, they heard about a franchise opportunity with a medium-sized parcel company, Hadron Couriers, based in Rugby. Hadron was looking to take on a franchisee to deliver to the north east of England. George made enquiries and, after looking at records provided by the company, calculated that there were already enough packages going from Hadron's central sorting depot to the north east for a franchisee to make a reasonable profit. If this was combined with income from taking items back from the north east on return trips, they would easily make the £35,000-£50,000 other franchisees were reportedly earning each year.

Donald was all for signing up as a franchisee and paying the £20,000 fee straightaway. He was impressed not only by the money-making potential of the business, but also felt the franchisor was a reputable company – a quoted plc, in fact – to work with. This was largely based on the fact that its chairman was well known for his charity fund-raising, chaired his local Conservative party and was a Freemason to boot. But George insisted on conducting due diligence, which involved taking references for the company and getting written replies to questions about its financial status. He also visited several existing franchisees he'd been referred to by Hadron, and even inspected their accounts.

George's research didn't uncover anything worrying about the company, so he and his father set up business in an industrial unit near the Rugby distribution point. But after just a couple of weeks a major problem emerged. George's father told him they were carrying such a high volume of parcels they needed to buy more vans. This should have been great news, except that George could see that their revenue was well below what they should have been making, given the mountain of items they were transporting.

It emerged that the parcels they were receiving hadn't been correctly weighed or their dimensions accurately measured by the franchisees that took initial delivery of them, before passing them on to the central depot and hence to George and Donald. These franchisees were understating their weight to reduce the charge to their customers. This helped win them business because it made them cheaper, and it didn't eat into their profit margin unduly because they only had to transport them a relatively short distance to Rugby. The real problem came when George had to get them all the way to the north east without getting adequate payment from the other franchisees.

When the pair complained to the franchisor, they were told that in future items would have their weight and dimensions verified at the depot, except that weeks later this still hadn't happened. And enquiries soon revealed theirs wasn't the only franchise losing money because of this dodgy practice, to which the franchisor was evidently turning a blind eye.

In an attempt to make their business profitable, the Ealings found local customers, who could be charged the official rate for the parcels. The problem was that any new customers had to be approved by the franchisor first. But after six months Hadron hadn't got around to approving any, despite the fact that George's business had now lost £80,000 thanks to the weights and measures issue.

As George became increasingly worried about his financial situation, he did further research into the franchise he'd signed up to.

He discovered that there was a very high turnover of franchisees, with stories of several mysteriously closing overnight. In addition, George found that certain senior figures at Hadron had serious criminal convictions, and that there were lawsuits pending against the company, which had not been disclosed during due diligence.

After nine months, to prevent their losses increasing, the Ealings put their business 'on hold' and suspended trading. They then started the process of taking Hadron to court to obtain compensation for numerous breaches of contract. Eventually, they won their case, but only after five very stressful years of struggling to avoid bankruptcy (by law, a bankrupt company cannot sue for compensation), which at one point saw them getting £400,000 in debt.

Looking back, George admits that the mistake he made was not doing enough checking on Hadron and its senior management. He eventually discovered, for example, that the books he inspected at the franchisees he'd been referred to by Hadron were doctored to make the businesses appear more profitable. What he should have done, he now knows, was to ask the company to recommend its top three franchisees, then ask who the next three were, and then ask for the three after that, and make those the ones he visited. (This technique should also be considered when obtaining references from prospective suppliers and service providers, such as accountants and web designers.)

At least George hasn't let his unfortunate experience with Hadron go to waste – he now advises entrepreneurs on how to set up and run successful businesses. And the biggest lesson he learnt from his foray into franchising? *'Having a strong, local network that you have taken the trouble to build up over several years is very important,'* he says. *'Only work with people you can trust who, ideally, have been recommended through your network.'*

⚠ There's no need to get the franchise agreement checked by a lawyer because it's non-negotiable.

It's true that there generally isn't much room for negotiation with these agreements, but you must still get a legal eagle to look at yours. If nothing else, he or she can make you aware of your obligations as a franchisee and highlight points in the contract that may need amending to fit your personal circumstances or where clarification should be sought from the franchisor.

It is not uncommon for companies to think they are selling a franchise when in reality they are offering no such thing. For example, a company may believe it is selling you distribution rights (which is a form of franchise), but really you are paying a fee plus royalties simply for the privilege of being someone's commission-only salesperson. You therefore need a solicitor who specialises in franchises to warn you and even advise walking away.

⚠ It's my franchise, so I can always sell it and get out if I feel like it.

Franchise agreements are legally binding and usually have iron-clad clauses limiting your opportunities for getting out early. You may find, for example, that you have to pay a hefty termination fee, or that you can't sell your franchise except to the franchisor for a sum well below its market value. So don't go into franchising on a whim.

⚠ Buying an existing business that has been trading for years must be low risk.

You can't make any assumptions about the viability of a business – after all, why would someone sell a successful firm in the first place? At least as much care and planning has to go into buying a business as buying a franchise. You'll need an accountant to go through the books, assessing its profitability and any liabilities it may have, such as unpaid debts. Meanwhile, a solicitor will have to get involved in putting together as favourable a deal as possible for you. For example, he or she may ask the vendors to warrantee assertions they make about the business. This means that if these turn out to be untrue, you can demand compensation from them.

You also need to decide how you will buy the business. Options include purchasing all its shares, just buying key assets of the business (this avoids the problem of taking on any debts it may have), or getting a loan from venture capitalists to buy a proportion of its shares (termed a management buy in, or a management buy out if you are already an employee of the company).

6

High Finance

Getting the money to start a business is seen by many wannabe entrepreneurs as the mountain that needs to be climbed before they can get started. If only they had the capital, they could turn their wonderful idea into a very profitable business.

In many ways this is a flawed view of start-up financing. Instead of regarding raising capital as something separate from your business, it may be more useful to see that the capital is the business. The amount of money you get, the way you get it and the terms on which it is given will often have a direct influence on the development of the new business. Likewise, the nature of the company you want to start will influence when, where and how you get your precious capital. A lack of appreciation of the interconnectedness of these two things, the business and the capital, is what leads to untold frustration for many start-ups. *'This is obviously a great business proposition, so why won't anyone give me money?'* they ask. Chances are they are looking in the wrong place for finance, given the kind of businesses they want to start.

It's also important to appreciate that financing your venture isn't likely to be a one-off event. You may need cash injections in the future to keep things on track even if you make a profit from day one. In fact, if you do very well, get lots of business and start to expand rapidly, you will almost certainly need more money. And what if the business gets off to a faltering start? How will you find the extra dosh to keep going until the business becomes more successful? Suddenly, financing your start-up can seem more like a mountain range you're constantly scrambling over, rather than a single peak. Are you prepared for that?

Alternatively, you may be lucky enough to have all the money you need already, perhaps from an inheritance or an investment windfall. The very important thing to remember here is that having money doesn't, on its own, make you an entrepreneur. In some ways, it is the struggle to get the money you need to start a business that turns you into a real business person. If you aren't able to actively raise the money to start your new business from external sources (a bank or investor, for example) then that could be an indication that you are no entrepreneur. Put another way, starting a business without going through the finance-seeking process removes an early, crucial test of your business abilities. Most importantly, you will have lost the chance to have third parties critically appraise your plans and tell you where they don't stack up.

I'll just have a word with my bank manager.

Banks are the first place many people think of when it comes to getting start-up money (Barclays Bank estimates it at one in four). After all, everyone knows they've got loads of the stuff and they're desperate to lend it out to make some profit, right? The key thing here is that the banks really do want to make a profit and definitely don't want to lose the money they've lent. But, you say, surely they're willing to take some risk to make that profit? The short answer, as many have found to their annoyance, is **no**. Knowing this fact, and understanding the reasons for it, can help tremendously with getting the money you need for your new company (be it from a bank or elsewhere). It can also alleviate a lot of the bewilderment, frustration and anger many feel when they fail to get that money.

Banks get a relatively modest return for their lending – they certainly aren't going to double their money overnight. This fact alone means that they must at all times minimise the risk of losing it. The easiest way to do this is to only lend when they can be sure of getting all their money back if things go wrong. In practice, this means a bank will typically expect you to raise finance from other sources and/or put up saleable assets (e.g. equipment or premises) as security which, combined, will match the money it will be lending the business. This immediately brings up a major problem for entrepreneurs: in order to get money, they need to have money (or assets) in the first place.

Having said that, some banks may relax the 50/50 rule for smaller loans – in the case of Barclays Bank £10,000 or under – or if you already have a personal account with them.

Unless your business idea is exceptionally straightforward, the bank will expect to see a business plan before it agrees to hand out any cash. Having to write a plan shouldn't, of course, even enter your mind as a reason not to consider a business loan (because you'll be writing a business plan anyway, won't you?). What might put you off, though, is the cost of the loan (arrangement fees, interest rates, etc.), repayment terms and any special conditions. Remember that with a business loan to a limited company or limited partnership, you, as a director, are not personally responsible for repayment of the debt should things go wrong. But you would be if you used a personal unsecured loan or remortgage of your home to finance your business.

When I asked Barclays Bank what puts its managers off providing start-up loans to people, I was told that having a criminal record wasn't necessarily a problem (as long as it wasn't fraud related). However *'the impression that a person has not thought through what he or she wants to do, isn't prepared, doesn't understand the business he or she is going into, is acting on a whim or is not putting any money in himself or herself'* were major turn offs, and understandably so. Interestingly, most of the new businesses Barclays helps are lifestyle, with only five per cent likely to become medium sized, reflecting the nature of start-ups in Britain today.

Ways to finance your start-up

There are four basic forms of finance for your new business: your own money, loans, outside investment and grants (which are covered at the end of this chapter). Each has its own set of advantages and disadvantages, and you may end up using a combination of them, or even all four. As a general rule, treat sources of finance (banks, private investors, venture capitalists, etc.) as you would any other 'suppliers' – talk to a number of them to get the best deal you can. →→→

Financing your start-up with **your own money** is an obvious first choice. For a start, you needn't ask anyone's permission to use it (except perhaps your other half) and it's a cheap option, in the sense that you don't have to pay arrangement fees or interest. Also, there won't be any annoying repayments which will eat into your gross profit. That said, are you prepared to risk a load of money it may have taken years of hard graft to accumulate? And if this capital is currently tied up in a lucrative investment, such as a property, can you be sure it won't do you more good where it is?

Think about what proportion of your money you want to risk in the venture, and how much you'll keep back in case things go wrong. That said, many successful entrepreneurs will tell you that it was only by being prepared to risk everything – and accepting that they could end up penniless and even bankrupt – that they were able to achieve ultimate success. Certainly, start-ups have a habit of sucking in money, and once you've spent a big proportion of your savings it can be difficult to resist putting in what you have left, rather than abandon a business that still isn't paying for itself. As one entrepreneur told me, *'When a company has lost you lots of money it feels easier to put in lots more, to try and turn it around. Ironically, it's only once it starts to make you money that you get reluctant to spend more cash on it.'*

The second option is to take out a **loan** (either personal or against the business). This is usually considered a cheap form of finance because it avoids the need to sell any part of your company to a third party (as is the case with investment finance). Its disadvantage is the lack of flexibility: you will need to make repayments on the loan whether your business is making a profit or not. This could leave you with no money to reinvest in the business to make it grow, or in the worst case lead to bankruptcy. If you are having difficulty repaying your loan, lenders may try to help you out, such as by giving you a repayment holiday, if they believe this is the best way for them ultimately to get their money back. However, all too often a

➔ ➔ ➔

disgruntled lender, such as a bank, will simply put a winding up order on your business in an attempt to recover their capital, which is something you never want to happen. All this means that debt financing can also be thought of as quite risky, especially if your financial planning hasn't enabled you to predict with much certainty your start-up's cashflow and profitability, so that you can't be sure of having the funds to pay off a loan.

This risk element is one of the reasons entrepreneurs often choose what may at first appear the least attractive finance option: **equity investment**. Put simply, this involves selling part of your new business to other people or businesses to obtain the money you need to get things going. In particular, if you have set up a limited company, then that company will issue shares (equity) in exchange for the investment. The total number of shares handed over will equate to an agreed percentage of the company that the investor wants for their money. For example, if an investor has asked for 50 per cent and there are already 100 shares in your company, an additional 100 shares will need to be created for the investor.

An obvious advantage of equity investment is that there is no interest charged on the money and there are no regular repayments. Better still, you are risking someone else's money rather than your own. In addition, having equity investors immediately gives your business added credibility (someone other than you or your gran thinks it can work), which can make it easier to get loans or further equity investment in the future. Chosen carefully, the investors themselves can prove an asset to the company by providing knowledge, experience and skills that you and your management team may lack. They can also act as mentors, helping you in your decision making and providing a sounding board for your ideas. But be aware that not all investors will be able or willing to help in this way. Many entrepreneurs are very reluctant to sell equity (in fact they often, erroneously, refer to it as 'giving away' a share of their company) and so miss out on its many advantages, financial and otherwise. The end result is often that they end up with a big share of a business going nowhere, rather than a smaller slice of a company making serious money. Which would you prefer?

Where to find equity investment

The first place many entrepreneurs look for investors is amongst friends and family (referred to within the start-up community as the 3Fs – the third F being Fools). These people will be naturally inclined to believe in you and your new venture, and so should be a relatively easy sell. They may also be as concerned with supporting you as they are about making lots of money. This means they may not look too closely at the details of your business idea (they may not even ask to see a business plan) and so might not fully appreciate the risks involved. As a consequence, they will ask for far less equity than any professional investor would at such an early stage in your start-up's development. All of which could have you thinking that your adoring (and wealthy) great aunt or your neighbour who won the lottery are the best people to start with. However, you may want to consider some of the disadvantages of using the 3Fs. For a start, you are now mixing your personal life with your business life, with all the associated complications. What if investor friends want to get closely involved in the running of the business – will you be able to tell them to back off? And if your business should fail, how will you feel about telling your brother that all the money he put into it – perhaps his life savings – is gone forever?

In investment terms, the next rung up from 3Fs are business angels. These are characterised as relatively wealthy individuals who are business savvy, have some knowledge of investment and are actively seeking out start-ups to invest in. To a budding entrepreneur, these people with their pots of cash (think tens of thousands of pounds, not millions) may well sound like candidates to be your new best friends. So where to find them? The fact is they can lurk anywhere, as there is no central registry of angels or particular organisation they all belong to.

Finding angels requires you to exploit all the contacts you've been making and the networking you've been doing as an important part of setting up your business. Saying that, there are some obvious starting points in your search, and these are the increasing number of regional angel networks that are being set up all around the UK. Each has a central contact point where you can find out more about the network. This includes how to submit your start-up's details for consideration by the networks' managers and co-ordinators, who – if they like what you're doing – will pass these on to network members or even invite you to make a presentation (for which some networks may charge a fee). But don't expect to be simply emailed a list of angels' names and phone numbers.

It's worth noting that angels often band together into syndicates to make their investments (this is separate to any networks they may also belong to). It benefits them because only one due diligence procedure has to be carried out (basically a check that all the things you've said are accurate) and only one contract needs to be drawn up, rather than a separate one for each angel investor. In fact, this may be the only way a small investor, with say £5,000 spare, could get a stake in a high-growth start-up. Having more money to play with – several hundred thousand pounds in some cases – also means they can get involved with a wider range of new businesses. The advantage for you is that you don't need to spend time negotiating with a bunch of individuals to get all the money you need, just the person heading the syndicate.

Finally, business angels get very tasty tax breaks for their investments through the Enterprise Investment Scheme (EIS), as long as the start-ups fit certain criteria – property investment, for example, wouldn't be a qualifying activity. To prove to investors that your business is okay for the scheme, you will need to obtain an EIS certificate from HM Revenue & Customs. Also, the tax man insists that angels be self-certified as either having a high net worth or being sophisticated investors. Someone could qualify for the latter by virtue of their professional experience (if they worked for an investment company in the City, for example) or simply by having been a member of an angel network for a few months. The intention of certification isn't, it would seem, to discourage people from investing, but merely to make them aware of the risks. It should also be pointed out that businesses can get the same tax benefits from angel investing as individuals. This little known scheme – Corporate Venturing – could conceivably open up some additional funding opportunities for you, such as family businesses looking to avoid corporation tax.

A source of even greater equity investment are the infamous **venture capitalists** (VCs). These people build multi-million-pound funds with money from, typically, very wealthy individuals for the express purpose of investing in high-growth companies. VC firms are pretty easy to find, with most belonging to the British Venture Capital Association (**www.bvca.co.uk**). Despite having 'venture' in their name, VCs are far from reckless with their investments. This can be a source of annoyance to some would-be entrepreneurs, who believe that they aren't prepared to take any risks at all, and only go for the 'safe bets'. In fact, even with all the care and effort they put into their investment decisions, VCs still reckon on a third of the businesses they invest in failing, and only a third providing a major return. As a rule of thumb, VC funding starts at the million pound level, as an investment less than this won't justify the considerable effort and cost involved in setting up a deal. They also tend not to invest in businesses that aren't yet trading, because a company without customers can't demonstrate there is a market for its product or service, and so is considered too high risk.

Another option you might consider for a more ambitious start-up is to form a **publicly quoted company** with shares traded on one of the smaller stock markets, such as London's Alternative Investment Market. Alternatively, you could have an offer for share subscription, which involves stockbrokers around the country asking their wealthier clients and investment funds to buy equity in your company. All shares stay private and are not traded on an exchange. This approach was particularly popular with hi-tech businesses during the boom years of the late Nineties, when everyone with a spare half-million quid was desperate to invest in this sector. However, there is a lot of regulation involved with share subscription offers, including producing an investors' prospectus (a detailed explanation of your business and what it plans to do with the money it raises), which can make them almost as expensive and time consuming as a stock market floatation.

When they hear my idea, big investors will immediately be queuing up to put money in my business.

You may well have a great business idea, but be under no illusions: selling equity to business angels and venture capitalists is not a quick and easy process. If your business plan hinges on getting outside investment, large or small, in a matter of weeks (rather than six months or more) then brace yourself for disappointment. The fact is there are lots of entrepreneurs with good ideas searching for start-up money every day. This means that investors can literally take their time to pick and choose where they put their cash. After all, if they do miss out on an opportunity, another one will always come along soon enough. And as with any deal in business, any hint of desperation is bound to be a real turn off. It is, therefore, vital you take account of the considerable time and effort required to raise equity finance when you start planning your venture. Even if you already have money from friends and family that's no guarantee a third party will be desperate to invest. As I've already said, 3Fs may be more interested in giving you support than getting a massive return on their money; outsiders will only be interested in a massive return. You should also remember that a good idea is not enough on its own to attract investment (see **Outside investment: getting your foot in the door**, (next page).

Business angels want to get involved with new businesses because they enjoy seeing them grow.

Don't be misled by the word 'angel' – these are hard-headed business people whose primary motivation is to make lots of money with their capital. It is better to think of them as what they really are, private investors – wealthy individuals putting their own hard-earned money on the line. After all, how philanthropic would you be if it were your life savings being entrusted to someone else's entrepreneurial abilities?

The angel label shouldn't imply these people are any more honest and trustworthy than anyone else. Always act with caution, don't take anyone at face value and never leave yourself vulnerable by putting undue trust in someone you hardly know. Talk to companies an angel has invested in before and generally ask around the angel networks. Also, don't take money from the first angel you talk to no matter how desperate you are – as ever, shop around for the best deal by talking to as many potential investors as you can.

 Investors will have to understand that I'm not going to sell off my business in a few years just to make them rich.

If that is your attitude, then don't even consider equity investment from VCs – and don't expect to instantly grab the attention of business angels either. These investors need to see as big a return on their investment as possible, and as quickly as possible, to justify the tremendous risk they're taking. This can only be done through an 'exit' whereby they dispose of their shares at a profit, which usually means either selling the business lock, stock and barrel to another company or a public flotation. Most angels and all VCs will not be interested in simply getting an annual dividend from the shares they have bought in your company, not least because there are much more secure ways to gain the level of income this would provide.

Outside investment: getting your foot in the door

Before doing anything, you must be sure that your business will naturally attract the attention of equity investors. As previously stated, it must definitely be a growth (rather than lifestyle) business. But to get real interest it must have the potential to grow enormously so that, typically, after four or five years angels and VCs can expect to see between a five and tenfold return on their initial investment. If this seems absurdly high, remember that the investors are putting their money into your business at the riskiest time, before it has been proven it will work. They could easily lose every penny and have nothing to show for it, so the reward has to be worth the risk.

Other factors that will make your business attractive include:

● strategic assets (for a developer this could be a plot of land in a prime location, and for a technology company registered patents)

● a USP that can't easily be copied or negated by a competitor

● operating in a growing market where demand can only increase

● already generating revenue

● proof of market demand for what you are selling, such as a high-profile 'trophy' customer

● potential to be the dominant player in your chosen market

● your absolute commitment to the venture. This could be by investing your own money, personally guaranteeing business loans or having spent a lot of time planning and developing the start-up (sometimes referred to as sweat equity). Be realistic, if you aren't prepared to risk anything in this business then why should anyone else?

It's unlikely you'll be able to tick all these boxes, but don't let that stop you looking for investment. However, if you have none, this may not be the right time. Remember, your objective when seeking equity funding is always to sell as little equity as possible to get the investment you need – as the investment professionals say, getting as high a valuation as possible for your business. (Perhaps the most famous example of getting this wrong was when Anita Roddick sold half of The Body Shop for just £3,000 pounds to a private investor to finance opening a shop. The investor eventually became one of the richest men in Britain when the company was floated, effectively at the expense of the Roddicks.) The more investor-attracting factors you have, then the higher will be your valuation. That's why it may be worth starting off using your own money, plus that of 3Fs and any loans you can get, and delaying selling major amounts of equity until you've filed your patents or secured your first big customers. And, as angels have a natural tendency to give higher valuations than venture capitalists, you might want to get funding to further develop the company from them before going to the VCs. (Angels usually resent the later involvement of VCs, who often get away with giving a lower valuation for the business than they did – even though the level of risk may have dropped.)

Your first practical step towards getting investment is to have a business plan designed to grab the attention of investors. Beyond what has already been said about writing it yourself, keeping it concise and giving it a punchy first page, it should also include specifics on the amount of money you need from investors, how investors might realise a return on that money and just how big that return is likely to be. You could even list companies likely to want to buy the company (what is called a trade sale – possibly to your competitors), potential private purchasers (which could be you and your fellow founders conducting a buyback) or stock markets where you could conduct an IPO (Initial Public Offering – the floatation of your company on, for example, the London Stock Exchange).

It should also be clear how you will structure and develop your company to make it attractive to a potential purchaser. You could point out how it will complement the business of the trade sale purchaser that you have identified, or what will make it a 'sexy' stock when floatation time comes. Potential investors will of course realise that this is largely conjecture (as illustrated by the fact that increasing numbers of VC-backed companies are now sold to other VCs, which their founders probably never predicted), but they will be impressed that you are at least thinking seriously about how you will eventually make them very rich. And if you have any customers already, be sure to mention this as it helps to prove there is a genuine market for your business.

Your business plan should also be tailored for the particular investors you will be sending it too. Some business angels, for example, may be keen to know how they can get actively involved in the running of the company (and if that's something you don't want, then don't approach such investors), but a VC will want to see that you have a strong management team already in place. In fact, if you are someone that the VCs and their contacts aren't going to know, and you have no demonstrable track record in business, then having senior managers committed to the company is vital. Even if these people, such as your financial director, are only involved on a part-time basis, they can still boost your venture's credibility with investors by appearing in the business plan. All of which brings us to the next point – save time and look more professional by only approaching suitable investors in the first place.

Most VCs specialise in particular business sectors, such as retail or hi-tech. Meanwhile, business angels and the networks they belong to will often only be interested in start-ups within a specific geographical region. You should be aware of these factors and use them when deciding who to approach for financing. If you find yourself blindly mass emailing your business plan to any organisation with money to invest, then you are either getting desperate (and as already stated, you should never appear desperate) or skimping on your research and preparation.

That said, you should still target a number of potential investors with your business plan, even if you think you have found one that would be a perfect match. It may turn out that a VC firm, for example, has already invested all of its latest fund but doesn't want to say 'no thanks' immediately, just in case you are the next Google or Starbucks. It could take weeks for it to finally decide it can't help you – time that could have been spent approaching other investors. And if you end up with a number of investors showing a serious interest, where's the harm? It could drive up the perceived value of your business as VCs and angels compete to invest in it.

Remember that your initial objective is to meet up with and present to a potential investor. You could be lucky and only have to make a few quick telephone enquiries then email your business plan to make this happen. However, be prepared to do a lot more. Even with the best business plan in the world, getting the attention of investors can be a very hit and miss affair. Indeed, some entrepreneurs say that approaching investors cold with a phone call, an email or by post has never worked for them. They only got anywhere when they used their network to get their business plan in front of investors' noses.

Okay, so the investors have received your business plan, they've somehow been induced to read it, they've been impressed by what they see... what next? Time to buy a new suit and tie...

I only want investors who will leave me alone and not interfere with my business.

Such 'silent partner' investors don't really exist. That's not to say all investors will want to get involved in the day-to-day running of the company. But most will want some say on the bigger decisions, such as a major capital purchase or the securing of further funding (which, if it is from another investor, might reduce their share of your business). At the very least, all investors have a right to be kept informed on the progress of the business through reports, annual accounts and an annual general meeting (although they'll probably want to see you more than once a year). In any case, investors, especially a carefully chosen angel, can be a good source of help and advice, and you should be planning to work with them, not ignore them.

⚠ I won't sell 20 per cent of my new business for anything less than £1 million.

What is anything – your car, your house, your dog, anything – actually worth? The simple answer is that it is worth what someone is willing to pay for it – end of story. This also applies to your start-up. What you think it is worth is irrelevant (even if you've used one of the recognised systems for calculating value, which are based on factors such as turnover and profit). That's not to say you shouldn't try to get the best deal you can, but holding out for an arbitrary figure in your head could mean that in ten years you have no investment and a 100 per cent share in nothing. Most importantly, don't put down any kind of company valuation in your business plan – it won't help you get the money you are after.

If you find it impossible to agree a valuation for your business, that doesn't necessarily mean an investment deal is dead. You can accept an investor's valuation but on condition that you regain a proportion of your business when he or she exits – as long as you have achieved the ambitious return that your investor was so dubious about at the beginning. Under the EIS, this arrangement can also be very tax efficient for the entrepreneur.

Investment brokers

Almost all entrepreneurs who believe passionately in what they are trying to achieve are capable of finding the funding they need themselves. That's not to say that everyone who looks for funding will definitely get it, but if you have a good business idea that you're able to present to others – investors, bank managers, development agencies, etc – in a compelling manner, then you stand a very good chance. (As I said in the Introduction, *Stupid Factor* is not a negative book!)

Despite that, when it comes to obtaining finance, there are people who are only too willing to help you – for a price. The fact is that these middlemen 'consultants' and 'business advisors' will not do anything you couldn't do yourself, whether it's approaching VCs or filling in an application for a bank loan. But that will not stop them from charging a fee for doing so. I have, therefore, formulated a golden rule to apply when dealing with such people: never pay any sort of up-front fee or a retainer (a monthly charge that has to be paid whether or not they have found suitable funding for you). If they are any good, they should be happy to make their money by taking a percentage of any funds they raise for you. End of story.

The sad fact is that there are unscrupulous individuals who make a living by seeking out and preying on vulnerable business people. These include entrepreneurs lacking in confidence or whose start-ups are in difficulty. Their trick is to get you to take a risk with them by offering the chance of salvation at a price, but without taking on any kind of risk themselves because they get paid a fee whatever the outcome. Unless someone is providing a well-defined professional service, such as a solicitor giving legal counsel or a priest praying for your soul, this fee-based arrangement only ever works to the benefit of one party – and trust me, that won't be you.

Having said all that, if you are looking for many thousands or even millions of pounds of financing, and you don't have the luxury of being able to wait indefinitely to find it, then it is understandable if you want to get some sort of professional help. In this case you might consider talking to an investment brokerage. A reputable one will only take on clients it thinks it can genuinely help, and it will not charge a large fee for doing so. The brokerage should know the best organisations to approach for the type of finance you're after and have personal contacts to ensure your application is taken seriously. Brokers should also make sure that you are presenting your proposition in the best possible light by polishing your business plan so that, for example, it's clear why you need equity finance rather than a bank loan.

If you are looking for equity investment, then brokers should be able to generate interest from a number of parties, which will help drive up the valuation of your business. They should also negotiate the best possible deal for you by acting as an intermediary between you and the investor. A less obvious benefit of this buffer role is that it can avoid ill feeling developing in the early rounds of negotiation, when investors tend to play tough. Finally, looking for investment is very time consuming (and comes on top of running your business and finding the new customers that will boost your valuation), so the brokerage can take some of that burden away from you. All of which may make you think that investment brokers are the obvious place to start looking for money. Alas, this help comes at a considerable price, namely a slice of any funding that is secured, but depending on your circumstances it may be a price worth paying.

It's easier to raise £1million than £50,000.

By now you should have realised that start-up capital is never easy to come by. So perhaps it is no surprise that if you ask an entrepreneur what is a 'good' sum of money to go after, they'll invariably give a bigger number than they are currently after. If they want £1million from venture capitalists, they'll say £5million is the magic figure; if they' re trying to scrape together £50,000 from business angels, then it's £250,000; getting £10,000 from the bank is tough, but £25,000 is no problem. This is only human nature – the money is always greener on the other side of the hill. But if you look hard enough, and take a flexible approach to the way you start your business and how you gather finance, there's money available to suit most start-ups around the UK. Indeed, a main function of regional development agencies and other state-funded grant providers, as well as some charities, is to plug perceived 'funding gaps' that exist in some parts of the country, for particular kinds of business or for certain groups in society.

You could simply ask for more money, but if that doesn't fit in with your business model and your financial projections, it could cause more problems than it solves. For example, if you're saddled with an unnecessarily large loan, your revenues may not cover the repayments. And if you ask potential investors for considerably more money than you require, they will simply demand more equity.

In any event, the sum of money you're after is not the key element; you, the business you want to start and, if you are looking for VC funding, your management team are the really important things. Get them right, and the start-up capital will follow.

Outside investment: closing the deal

Okay - your business plan has been read by investors who now want to find out more. That means having a formal meeting, about an hour long, where you and your management team present the business idea, provide further detail of your plans and answer specific questions regarding your proposal. This will be done in front of partners in the VC firm, the manager of the angel network or individual private investors, depending on who you're chasing for money.

Professional investors, especially VCs, meet with start-ups all the time, and have heard it all before. You really need to think about how you can stand out from the crowd and sell your proposition to them.

A good idea is to have a strong opening to your presentation where you let them know straightaway what is sexy and exciting about your business. (But as one entrepreneur told me, avoid throwing your arms around and shouting when talking to VCs – they're often accountants and scare easily.) Don't be surprised if it seems the investors haven't got beyond the first page of your business plan: acting dumb could be a way for them to see how your team reacts under pressure. And don't be caught out by questions like 'why should I invest in you?', 'how many phone calls do salespeople have to make to sell one item?' and

'what would you do if we gave you more money than you've asked for?' or a request to 'summarise your business in one sentence'. Be prepared for anything!

It is important that you spend time practising your presentation so that on the big day you will come across as focused on your venture, knowledgeable about the market it will be operating in and capable of strategic thought. (Deals are only struck by businesses that are seen as both attractive and prepared.) Your ultimate objective is to leave the investors feeling confident about your team and the money making potential of your start-up – confident enough to give you lots of money.

After the meeting, if the investors are still interested, they will see who else is active in your market (very few business ideas are so original that there's no competition at all). They will want to talk to any customers you may already have and also investigate the novel aspects of your business. For example, if you are a hi-tech start-up they will look at your technology and intellectual property – patents and registered designs. There may be further meetings before the investors make their final decision, which will come down to their personal opinions as much as anything else. If they don't think your team is strong enough and aren't sure there's enough of a market for what you're doing, they'll walk away. Likewise, if you aren't attracted to your potential investors, don't overlook this in your desperate attempt to get money. You will be stuck with your investors for years to come, so you need to be able to get along with them. You may also want investors to provide not just cash but help and advice, which, as I've stated before, not all are willing or able to do.

Even once the investor of your dreams has agreed to put money into your venture, that doesn't mean the hard work is over. You will need to negotiate the amount of equity you are willing to hand over. The investor (particularly a VC) is likely to be far more experienced at this game than you, so you'll need all the help you can find at this stage. This could be experienced business people – CEOs (chief executive officers), company chairmen, financial directors – that you know or who you have collected along the way in your hunt for money. In fact, you will find many business people take great pleasure in helping start-ups and will be more than happy to provide free advice. Be aware, taking lots of advice will slow down the negotiation process, as you have the investor's various assertions regarding the business assessed by your team of helpers.

Will Franks is part of a management team that secured first round equity investment for the technology start-up UbiquiSys. He describes the final stages of securing funding, after over seven months of searching: *'It was nerve racking as the VC seemed to string out the whole thing even after we'd got our term sheet [the investment offer and its terms]. We had to remember that the deal could still be lost, so we needed to be on the ball at all times. This last stage can be a painful experience – you are mortgaged to the hilt and struggling to keep going until the investment money comes in, but the VC just doesn't realise he is pulling the strings of a team that feels in the dark and on tenterhooks.'*

In the event that several investors want to invest, you will receive a term sheet from each one. It will then usually be a matter of picking the offer with the highest valuation for your company, although the terms of the offers and also the chemistry between you and the various investors will also be important.

Business angels

Be on the lookout for angels who are really just looking for a job with your company. That may not be a problem if he (and it almost always is a he – usually in his mid-forties to early fifties and divorced) can complement your existing management team. But if the job he would take is one that's already been filled by you or one of your founding directors, then that could cause problems. Also, beware of demands for expensive due diligence, as the relatively small amount of money business angels will be putting in your business could soon get swallowed up by this (angels usually do their own due diligence, at minimal cost). Similarly, avoid over-complicated angel deals, such as those in which directors earn back equity in their company each year by achieving turnover targets (which is not to be confused with the equity on exit scheme mentioned previously). Getting a solicitor to properly word a convoluted agreement can be costly and they ultimately do nothing to actually help the business. Another thing to look out for is an angel providing investment in the form of a loan to be repaid. This is a case of an investor having their cake (a share in your company) and eating it (getting their money back even if your company is still struggling to be a success). Having said that, a VC will definitely have lots of cake-and-eat-it elements in their deal (what is called downside protection), some of which you will invariably have to accept.

I can quickly draw up an agreement on a side of A4.
Saying something like this in a meeting with investors will kill a deal dead, even if everything up to that point has been going brilliantly. You will look like a naive fool and all your credibility will evaporate. Any agreement with investors must be drawn up using legal counsel, not least to protect yourself. This will, of course, cost money, so that very small investments may not be worth the trouble. (Business angel deals, for example, are not usually for less than £25,000.) And even if you don't hire a solicitor, you can rely on the investors having a legal pit bull in their corner.

The company will definitely not need any more money to grow.

Optimism can be a virtue when you're starting out in business, but, as in this case, too much risks being a Stupid Factor. Your business plan may well show your start-up can get going and become profitable with a single loan or one round of equity investment, and that it can grow just using its profits. But you must be prepared for things not going to plan by being able to access extra funds as required. This could be as simple as arranging an overdraft facility with your bank, even if you never intend to use it. Or it may mean always being on the lookout for potential investors, or choosing your initial investors on the basis that they have extra funds that can be called upon if required. Certainly, experienced investors will always assume that a new, high-growth company will need further financing in the future, whatever the plan says.

 ### I'll only need outside investment if there's a problem, so I won't waste time thinking about it now.

The words 'investment' and 'problem' do not sit well together. A crisis is a bad time to look for investment; any new business represents a big risk for investors, but one that's already having difficulties is an enormous gamble. If there is any reason to believe that the money you have to start the business won't be enough to see it through to profitability, then think about outside investment sooner rather than later. Yes, taking on outside investors when there's a chance you can make the company work without them could itself seem like a gamble – you may end up having 'given away' part of your business needlessly. But given the advantages of equity investment for your start-up (enhanced credibility with third parties such as banks; advice and practical assistance from the investors themselves), selling part of your company as an insurance against future difficulties may prove to be the smarter move. And doing it when things are going well will, ironically, be the best time as you'll get the highest valuation. So when you get your first customers, that may be the moment to think about getting outside money, not convince yourself that initial sales will be enough to get your company through the critical first 18 months.

CASE STUDY: Ultroxmedia

Ken Worthington had worked for years as an administrator in a large financial services company. But being a small cog in a big corporate machine wasn't making him happy – and so one day he decided he'd had enough and simply left his job, without another one to go to. This dramatic step eventually led to him getting a masters degree and then starting up a business with some like-minded friends.

This company did a random assortment of multimedia and web work, and even turned a profit, but it had no real focus. Unhappy with this ad hoc approach to business, Ken soon left to co-found Ultroxmedia with his programmer wife and the managing director from the previous company. But Ultroxmedia also lacked a goal and a business plan – instead, the founders would simply see what ideas came along that they could use as the basis for their new venture.

One such idea was a software product, Prexapro, which would help businesses create multimedia presentations. Importantly, these presentations would be held in a library in such a way that staff, such as salespeople, could retrieve them as required, but they would only be able to make limited changes to the individual slides that made up the presentation. This would tackle the serious problem of staff amending presentations as they saw fit, and often going against a company's rules about corporate style and content.

Prexapro would provide an attractive alternative to using CD-ROMs to provide tamper-proof presentations. Any change to a presentation on a CD-ROM requires new CDs to be created and distributed, often at considerable cost. But with the library system, where the slides are held on a computer hard drive, the only cost would be having individual slides changed by Ultroxmedia, which would create all the slides in the first place.

With a prototype version of Prexapro that was adequate for demonstrations, Ultroxmedia began marketing it by telephoning the marketing departments of large companies. It was found to be a tough product to sell over the phone – not least because it wasn't easy to explain what it did in just a few sentences to a total stranger. Nevertheless, a year after setting up the business, their first major customer came into view – an international insurance group. (Insurance companies are particularly wary of salespeople amending presentations because by doing so they could easily break the many regulations governing this industry. They could also compromise a company's precious brand image by, for example, altering logos and strap lines.)

Even though the insurance company was very keen on the product, it demanded an extensive evaluation before it would adopt Prexapro. This meant that it took months to get from initial enquiry to final sale – which proved frustrating for the staff at Ultroxmedia, as well as putting a major strain on its finances. Even when the final contract was signed, the customer was very slow at paying invoices, which resulted in serious cashflow problems for Ultroxmedia. This, in turn, meant it couldn't put together a serious marketing budget.

Nevertheless, with such a high-profile client finally on board, Ken and his colleagues felt the sky was the limit for their start-up – with its growth financed by the revenue from the insurance group and the other big names that would surely soon follow. Then disaster struck – there was a management shake-up in the marketing department at the insurers which resulted in a number of its suppliers being dropped, including Ultroxmedia and Prexapro. There was nothing wrong with the product, but without someone championing its cause at the very highest tier of management it simply didn't survive a major reorganisation, despite the fact that the corporation had spent over £160,000 on it. It was just one of those things that can happen when dealing with big companies – and that small suppliers can be almost powerless to do anything about.

So now Ultroxmedia was back at square one, trying to sell a very novel product that nobody was currently using. It tried to push Prexapro through design agencies, but despite setting up a promising partnership, this didn't lead anywhere. Agencies, it seemed, found it hard to commit themselves to pushing this particular product to their clients.

With money running low, Ken tried to find outside investment. This included giving presentations to venture capitalists using a business plan vetted by a major accounting firm at a cost of £5,000.

(This expense was met by a grant. The accountants' main contribution was an Excel spreadsheet used to calculate cashflow, except that it was found to contain errors in its equations which Ultroxmedia had to correct.) But none of this effort won any new investment and Ultroxmedia was forced to close, after four-and-half years of hard work. This was despite the fact that *'some big names were interested and success never seemed far away.'*

How could such a good idea, with a proven demand, end up going nowhere? Why did Ultroxmedia fail? *'The minute we got the insurer on board we should have gone for VC money,'* says Ken. *'But frankly, we were resentful that when we really needed help nobody wanted to know. We thought that surely, with three of us in the company working hard and money coming in from the insurer, we could succeed on our own.'*

But even if the insurer had remained a client, outside funding would still have been required. It was now obvious that effectively marketing this specialist product wouldn't be easy and required considerably more capital. Prexapro was most likely to appeal to big companies, and as the team had already discovered, selling to these people is a longwinded process, plus they tend to be very slow payers. So even if another juicy customer was soon found, this wouldn't do anything to help Ultroxmedia's cashflow for many months. Not looking for investment as soon as it had a prestige customer was always going to lead to difficulties in the longer term. Ironically, the perfect time to look for help was when things had never been better.

Grants

Yes, there really is serious money being handed out free to businesses – but don't expect that getting your hands on it will be as easy as a trip to the cash machine. That's because strict rules are applied as to who is eligible for this dosh and for what purposes it can be used.

The most important grant issuing bodies these days are the Regional Development Agencies (RDAs). As the name implies, these are responsible for distributing funds from a range of government agencies and the European Union to businesses within particular areas of the country. The total amount of money they have to hand out relates to how economically deprived their patch is considered to be. In addition, specific zones within a region may be deemed in particular need of assistance, so that further funds are made available.

The principle aim of an RDA is to bring employment and economic prosperity to its region, which is reflected in the criteria it uses for deciding which businesses can receive what grants. If you are looking to get a large grant for your business, don't expect this to be a quick and easy process – let's face it, they can't dish out money that never has to be paid back to just anyone, can they? Your business may also be expected to match money provided to fund, say, research and development for an innovative product, or staff training.

There are small grants of up to £1,000 available for very specific purposes, such as leadership and management training or website development. These grants are unlikely to be the foundation stone of your start-up, but can certainly help it on its way and are relatively straightforward to obtain. The best starting point for finding out what grants are currently available in your area is your local Business Link or RDA.

Government-funded grants also become available within particular industries, and are not tied to a particular region. You are likely to find out about these through your industry grapevine, by approaching central government agencies or through official centres of excellence. Some charities also issue grants, the most high-profile example being the Prince's Trust (**www.princes-trust .org.uk**), and it's also worth considering entering business competitions, such as Shell Springboard (**www.shellspring board.org**). These should be approached directly to find out what funds are available and what kinds of businesses are eligible.

A particularly important form of 'grant' for start-ups is the DTI's Small Firms Loan Guarantee Scheme, which helps provide financing for businesses that can't find the money they need anywhere else. It involves obtaining a bank loan (it need not be from the bank you have your business account with), 75 per cent of which is guaranteed by the DTI in the event that your business fails. A bank will not demand that you have assets to underwrite the loan, but you must show that you can repay it out of cashflow (i.e. enough money will be coming in each month to cover the repayments). There's a big variation in how banks view these loans, and the charges associated with them can be quite high, so be prepared to talk to several bank managers to get the deal you want. And don't leave your application to the eleventh hour – the approval process can take months.

Prof Birchall says:

When it comes to grants, there is a big danger of 'initiative overload', with money coming through a range of sources, including the RDAs, in lots of small parcels. It's a jungle out there, and business people have difficulty finding their way through it. What's more, there are hurdles for start-ups and SMEs in getting access to this money, not least because of the narrow criteria they must meet. It's not unfair to say that businesses can be made to jump through hoops to obtain this funding. A judgement has to be made whether you would be better off talking to your next customer rather than filling in the often quite difficult forms. Put another way, you need to weigh the potential benefits against the opportunity costs. Even here at Henley we often find it hard work to secure European Union funds for the development of new initiatives.

So if you have a good idea for a business you should try not to be too distracted by the possibility of grants. Having said that, if these are your only source of funds because you can't find any other backers, you may not have much choice in the matter. And, while not wanting to contradict my earlier comment about hoop jumping, in some ways hurdles aren't a bad thing – being forced to put your idea on paper and then having your assumptions questioned when applying for a grant can be surprisingly useful.

It's worth noting that it is not always to the advantage of grant givers to have too many applications flood their post box, as this increases the time and cost involved in allocating the funds. Therefore, some grants may be poorly promoted – so keep your eyes peeled for the more attractive opportunities.

7

Start-up Stories: Timing is Everything

In this chapter, we'll look at two Internet-based technology companies, both concerned with messaging in its various forms. One got everything right from the start – it identified a potentially profitable market, created a strategy for attacking it and developed a product tailored to meet its needs. The only trouble was that its timing was way off, so even having talented people doing good work wasn't enough to prevent it going bump overnight.

The founder of the second company got a lot of things wrong from day one, making life very difficult for himself in the process. But somehow the business managed to keep going, and is now in real danger of being a success. Indeed, it may well prove that his timing was spot on, making up for all the other Stupid Factors he blundered into.

e-go systems

Ian Roberts is what some would call a serial entrepreneur. His first business involved the buying and selling of supermarkets, and proved very successful. Ian followed this up with something rather different: a voice messaging service for companies that needed to maintain two-way contact with a mobile workforce, principally salespeople (this was in the days before the near-universal use of mobile phones). With a turnover of £1 million in the UK and Ireland this proved reasonably successful, but as it served a niche market there wasn't much opportunity for further growth.

Simultaneously, the Internet was beginning to enter the public consciousness, and Ian realised that this provided a means for delivering a fuller messaging service to businesses. While Ian was very knowledgeable about the technology market as a whole, this idea strayed into areas that were new to him. Consequently, he consulted with technical experts who could confirm if his idea made sense – and on the whole they believed it did. This was back in 1998 when it was by no means certain that the Internet, along with the technology behind it, would become such a universal means of communication. But Ian bet that it would. He also believed, along with many others, that broadband would become readily available to businesses over the next few years, which was crucial to his business plan (for reasons that will become evident further on in this case study). And so 'e-go systems' was born, to exploit the Internet to provide better messaging for companies.

It would do this by providing Universal Messaging (UM). This is where you access all your messages – fax, email, voice mail, text – in one place, such as a website or by dialling a phone number and hearing emails read back to you by a computer. Its purpose is twofold: to save time (you aren't wandering between your answering machine, fax and PC all day), and to provide better messaging communications when you are out of the office. While UM was not a new concept in itself, providing it to businesses over the Internet certainly was. Moreover, e-go would use an ASP model for delivering this service. What's that? An ASP (Application Service Provider) provides a service without your having to buy and maintain lots of software and computer hardware yourself. Instead, the ASP takes care of all that, while you access the service from the comfort of your desktop computer through the Internet. Hotmail is a relatively simple example of an ASP service, with all the important software being held on Microsoft's computers, not yours. The ASP model was important for e-go because that would allow it to sell its service to SMEs – organisations without the money and resources to buy a UM service they would have to house and maintain themselves.

As you might guess, developing a whole new technology,

combining UM, ASP and a bunch of other scary acronyms wouldn't be easy, quick or cheap. So before going hell for leather, Ian conducted a 'proof of concept' pilot project that would show all this techno-babble could be turned into something real that worked. This project was also vital to help establish what the market was for this service. And so e-go's first round of funding, which totalled £5million, was directed to achieving these twin goals. (It is normal practice for investment money to be obtained in chunks or 'rounds'. Trying to obtain ALL the money you might need to become a fully functioning, profitable business in one go is a tall order even in the best of circumstances.)

This initial investment was raised through an offer for share subscription (see page 92), which is like a share floatation except that the shares stay privately owned and cannot be publicly traded on a stock exchange. (At this time, UK venture capitalists were still not taking a big interest in Internet-based businesses, though all that was to change after the massive success of Freeserve.) Much of the money raised by Ian went on hiring a quality management team as well as programmers and telecommunications specialists to actually develop the UM prototype. This was eventually demonstrated to two important telecommunications companies, US giant AT&T and Telia. They liked what they saw (or more accurately, what they heard, as they were given a demonstration of voice messaging using Internet technology), and gave feedback on what features they would like to see in a finished version of the system. More importantly, they committed themselves to marketing the finished version to their customers – and so the marketing model for e-go systems was born.

It was decided that it would be impractical and too expensive for e-go to market its service direct to end users. Instead, telecommunications companies would distribute and sell it for them. This made particular sense as a whole new bunch of telecoms companies were poised to hit the market when British Telecom finally got around to introducing broadband Internet access throughout the UK. (The liberalisation of the telecommunications market in the UK meant BT had to allow other telecoms companies to make use of any broadband services it introduced.)

Following this very positive development, Ian went back to his financiers and explained that more money was now needed to get the UM prototype working on an industrial scale. This meant that it would function with an unlimited number of people using it, as well as having all the extra features requested by the telecoms companies. This resulted in a second round of financing in 2001 which netted £7.5million, mainly from the same private investors. (Given that this happened after the tech bubble had burst, it was no mean achievement, and involved painting an exciting picture of what new things could be achieved once the basic system was established.)

e-go soon had trial customers using the advanced prototype, and staff numbers began to swell as a small army of salespeople and others were taken on in advance of a big marketing push for the completed version. But then disaster struck: the technology couldn't be scaled up. When it was used by more than a few people at a time, the system crashed. Investigations revealed that this was because the interface technology that allowed telephone voice messages to be put onto the Internet was inadequate. This had been supplied by a technology partner that had assured Ian it was up to the job, and e-go was left with no choice but to reinvent the interface from scratch (e-go eventually won considerable compensation from the original interface supplier). Ian had to inform investors of this new problem (thus harming the company's reputation with them), including the fact that nobody knew how long it would take to fix.

In fact, a working version of the new interface was ready six months later. During this time, e-go had expensive sales and marketing staff who, despite being very busy talking to customers, weren't in a position to close any deals and bring in any much needed revenue. This meant the company used up its investment capital much faster than anticipated. Worse still, e-go's market was beginning to evaporate.

BT had been slower than expected to introduce broadband services, so that most of the new telecommunications companies that were going to sell e-go's UM service were forced to close down. Even the big, established telecoms operators now faced financial difficulties – along with plummeting share prices – and were only interested in keeping their core business alive. Selling 'value added' services, including UM, no longer interested them.

The crunch came when e-go tried to win a major contract with a top UK corporation developing a new hi-tech service incorporating UM. Ian's company clearly demonstrated it had the best offering (it had beaten IBM in an earlier stage of the tendering process), boasted an excellent list of industry partners and had £37.5million of loan funding pending as proof of its financial stability. But even with all this, e-go failed to win the business, as the customer chose to play it safe and go with a better known name – BT. There was now no alternative but to accept the fact that a company that has no customers and is unable to win customers also has no future, and that taking up further funding wouldn't alter that. Within a week, e-go had closed down and its workforce been made redundant.

How did a good idea end up going so wrong, despite thorough planning, the recruitment of an excellent management team, and the eventual development of first rate technology, albeit with some hiccups along the way? In retrospect, e-go was in a vulnerable position from the start, building a new technology (UM over the Internet) for an unproven end market (did SMEs want UM?) provided through resellers (the new telecoms companies and alternative broadband service providers) that weren't themselves fully established. To cap it all, e-go was reliant on a development – broadband Britain – that was in the hands of a company that had little financial incentive to make this happen (broadband, in the form of ADSL, would take money away from BT's very profitable leased line business). All this was compounded by the fact that e-go couldn't make any money until it got to the end of a long and expensive cycle of product development, not to mention a lot of marketing.

The irony is that Ian was fully aware of these risks. As he says, *'All the factors that eventually brought e-go down were identified in our shareholder's prospectus. Unfortunately, all of these were out of our control – it was definitely the timing we got wrong.'* And the lessons leant? *'When the market moves against you, you need to be able to reengineer your company quickly. And if you're not making a profit, you need to make decisions fast and early.'*

MaserMessaging

Imagine you run a shift operation, perhaps on a production line or in a hospital, and some of your employees, without warning, simply don't turn up for work one day. What do you do? Chances are you need all the employees you were expecting to turn up to work a particular shift (the days of having staff to spare are long gone). You may even need a minimum number of staff present for statutory reasons if your business is in the caring sector. One solution would be to try calling your other employees to see who is available at short notice. But this takes time, may involve awkward conversations as you try to convince reluctant workers to drop what they're doing and come to work, and may not even be possible if you don't have people's up-to-date contact numbers. Little wonder then that many businesses turn to using staff supplied by an agency – despite the fact you are charged a hefty premium for everyone they send. Wouldn't it be better if there was a more efficient system for calling on your existing staff?

This question was the starting point for Adam McClelland's start-up, MaserMessaging. He envisaged an automated service that companies could subscribe to, which used messaging technology – email and, more importantly, text messages – to get the extra staff they needed, when they needed them. (The availability of a text service is particularly important: you can't rely on all employees having access to the Internet, but nearly all will have a mobile phone.) MaserMessaging would be responsible for keeping a record of employees' email addresses and mobile phone numbers, so that these wouldn't be disclosed to the employer (which eliminated any possibility of staff being bullied into working). Also, the system could be activated by the employer with just a text message (or by email or through a website), and employees could indicate on the system their availability for work in the same way. The system would be quick, efficient and very cost effective, and all Adam had to do now was turn it from a nice idea into something real. Did I say that was all he had to do?

Before founding MaserMessaging Communications Ltd, Adam

had worked for 15 years in mergers and acquisitions, and before that he'd been a manager in the food industry – which is where he acquired his appreciation for the difficulties of managing shift work. Significantly, he had no technical background and was definitely no computer whiz-kid, and so needed to find someone who could turn his golden vision into nuts and bolts reality.

After talking to several software developers, he found one who seemed ideal. Firstly, he understood what Adam was trying to achieve (not everyone he spoke to grasped the basic idea of MaserMessaging), he had most of the required competency and he was immediately available to work as a contractor. He would charge £36,000 per year for his time and he reckoned the project would take 18 months. This led Adam to calculate that the total cost of developing, launching and marketing MaserMessaging would be £100,000 – money he could find out of his savings. So with the financing easily sorted, Adam contracted the programmer, rolled up his sleeves and got started, founding a limited company with himself as the only major shareholder.

Adam spent a lot of time during the development stage talking to potential customers, and finding out in detail what features they would want to have in such a messaging system. These comments were fed back to the programmer who then, to his frustration, had to amend his work accordingly. As a consequence, it took nearly two-and-a-half years to initially develop the service.

When the product development was finally completed it came time to do the first live demonstration in front of a potential customer. But what should have been a moment of pride and triumph soon turned to embarrassment as the new system failed to work. The problem, it was soon established, lay with the database element of the system, which worked far too slowly to be of any use.

After over two years of effort, and with nothing commercial to show for it, things were now looking very tough for Adam and his company. His contractor was unable to rectify the problem, and being a one-man band, this person had no one to turn to for help. At the same time, money was starting to get tight as development had taken longer than expected and there were still no revenues.

At this time Adam was approached by a group of consultants who offered to help him manage MaserMessaging. They said they would write a business plan and use it to help him find extra financing, including investors. They would also act as a 'surrogate board of directors', providing general guidance and advice. Adam liked what they had to say and, despite having difficulty paying even his household bills, took them on, at a fee of £1,500 per month.

On the technical side, relief came when Adam's consultants put him in contact with a development house whose programmers had a reputation for speed and quality. And they lived up to this when they took Adam's system and built a fully functioning version of it for him from scratch. And the real shocker? They did this in one week.

It should be pointed out that the effort that Adam and his contractor went to over the previous two-plus years was not completely in vain. To have used a proper development house from the beginning, with Adam constantly amending his specification for the system, would have been cripplingly expensive. If nothing else, through the earlier work he had been able to give the new programmers an exact specification to work from, and thus made absolute best use of their very expensive time.

On the finance side, things went from difficult to desperate as Adam was forced into remortgaging his home. However, some relief came in the form of a business angel investor introduced to Adam by his consultants, who would provide both much needed investment capital and help with marketing. This was the only potential investor he had spoken to, and though he knew the angel's valuation for the company was miserly, Adam readily sold him 25 per cent of the company for £50,000 (although days after doing this he found someone who would have been willing to give him the same money for just 12½ per cent). But almost from the start, things didn't go well with the investor, who seemed more interested in getting high-salaried marketing jobs in MaserMessaging for his mates than providing any real assistance. Soon, with a growing feeling of mistrust, the relationship between Adam and the investor broke down altogether. The situation was only resolved when Adam bought back the angel's shares at a premium, which was yet more expense he could have done without.

The consultants' next suggestion was that Adam should take out a bank loan through the Small Firms Loan Guarantee Scheme. They would assist with setting up meetings with the bank and handling all the red tape. Adam decided to do this and after a few months secured a life-saving £100,000.

But hang on – finding dodgy investors, sourcing suppliers, getting a bank loan: why would anyone pay high-powered consultants to help them do all this? Surely, all this can be done by any entrepreneur – without expensive third-party assistance. After all, there's a wealth of help and good advice to be had out there for little or no cost. So why?

'I thought it would all be a lot harder than it really was,' is Adam's answer. In fact, soon after getting the loan money, he started to find investors on his own initiative – friends and associates who could supply technical knowledge and business savvy, as well as money. It soon became obvious that he no longer needed the help of his retained consultants – if, in fact, their help had ever really been required.

With a viable service, new funding and a proper board of directors, McClelland was finally able to start winning business – which soon included some prestige names. But he is the first to admit he is no salesman; cold calling managing directors and convincing them they need a whole new service does not come naturally to him. Even his intimate knowledge of and passion for MaserMessaging doesn't overcome this talent gap. The failure to deal with this issue from the outset is accepted by Adam as having limited the growth of the company. *'I should have learnt more about selling early on,'* he admits. *'Not necessarily with formal training, but by talking to experienced salespeople.'*

Things are now looking very positive for Adam's firm, as it wins more clients. *'The service has a wow factor that gets even the most cynical managers excited when it is demonstrated to them,'* he says. In addition, the core service is being adapted so it can be sold into new areas – for example, it can now be used by businesses to quickly tell their customers about last-minute offers. And the next major step, Adam believes, will be to secure venture capital funding for further growth.

However, it is important to assess the cost involved in reaching this stage, which totalled over £300,000 – most of which came straight from the managing director's pocket and drove him to the brink of bankruptcy. This included spending £10,000 on the services of a patent agent to register a patent for the company's messaging system, and almost £5,000 on drawing up the shareholders' agreements. Then there was the £70,000 spent on marketing, most of which went on Adam McClelland travelling the country doing demonstrations and meeting potential business partners, and taking stands at exhibitions. It also covered the cost of employing a sales lead generator who cold called potential customers – though this tactic was soon dropped when it brought no business.

As I investigated the story of MaserMessaging, I couldn't help thinking that many of its difficulties came from the fact that Adam was working in an area – messaging technology – he was totally unfamiliar with. But Mr McClelland refuses to accept this, declaring: *'If you've got a good idea, follow it!'*

The final message

Ian, an experienced and successful entrepreneur, knew that for e-go to stand a chance he needed a strong management team around him, to handle both the commercial and technical aspects of what he was trying to achieve. He also needed to secure financing appropriate to the magnitude of the task in hand. Adam, however, through a lack of experience and a self-confessed desire to save money and retain equity in his company, allowed himself to believe that he was the only senior manager or director his company needed. This was despite his having no familiarity with the complicated process of software development. Almost certainly, having a technical expert as a company director early on, instead of stoically going it alone, would have saved him considerable time and money. This person might have pointed out the importance of talking to potential customers to create a detailed specification for the technology you want to create before any major investment in development. In fact, Adam admits that if he had done this, and had used a development house instead of a lone contractor, he could have had his service ready at least six months earlier. More importantly, it would have greatly reduced the very real risk of MaserMessaging failing before it had even got its first customer. But at least one thing was in Adam's favour – timing. He appears to be offering a service that customers are now getting excited about and which, as yet, has no direct competition.

But as Ian Roberts states, the timing was problematic for e-go: if he had waited for all the identified risk factors to resolve themselves, particularly the roll out of broadband Britain by BT, he would have entered the market too late, with his competition already established so that there would be less money to be made. By taking a greater risk and going early, he instead hoped to have the market all to himself, which would have brought enormous rewards. For a high-growth start-up, balancing risk and reward is what timing is all about.

Why, you may ask, did some messaging companies survive the bursting of the technology bubble while others, such as e-go, went under? In 1999, just as e-go was developing its UM/ASP offering, a little-known company in Canada, RIM, was launching its own messaging service, BlackBerry. This also enabled employees to get emails when they were out of their office, but in this case they were received automatically on a battery-powered pocket device. It is tempting to think that such an obviously great idea was always destined to succeed, whatever happened. But as has been mentioned before, on its own a good idea never guarantees success – what is also needed is an effective way of attacking a carefully identified market.

In the case of BlackBerry, its market was almost exclusively big corporations to begin with, that already possessed the equipment and the technicians needed to make the messaging system work. This meant RIM could grow its BlackBerry business gradually, one high-value customer at a time, without undue dependence on factors outside its control. On the other hand, e-go was selling mainly to SMEs, each of which would need help setting up the UM service, despite the use of the ASP model – hence the reliance on soon-to-disappear telecoms companies to do this on e-go's behalf. Also, e-go couldn't be content growing one customer at a time. Once its UM system was in place it needed to win a lot of relatively low-value customers quickly to cover its costs, which, once it started to lose its 'route to market', made it much more likely to fail.

8

The Professionals

You may have got through your life up to now without talking to a single accountant or solicitor, but all that will quickly change once you go into business (unless you are running the most straightforward of sole trader operations). Dealing with these people can be a daunting prospect – many new entrepreneurs worry that they may not speak a language they understand and will charge a fortune. But if they are chosen carefully, these people needn't bamboozle you with lots of jargon, and there are ways of working with them that will cushion the expense. In any case, sometimes you will have no option but to call on the services of a boring bean counter or a lofty lawyer.

In this chapter we will look at a number of issues surrounding these two professions. This includes examining some common misconceptions regarding contract law and intellectual property (copyright and patents).

A contract must be written down to have any legality.
Generally, a verbal contact is as legally binding as a written one (a particular exception being a house purchase). Of course, in the event of a dispute, it may be harder to prove the existence of a verbal contract or exactly what its terms were, which is why you should always have a written contract. It's also worth noting that for an agreement to constitute a legal contract it must be a two-way street – I will do something for you (such as pay some money) only if you do something for me (such as provide a product or service). For example, if you were to say to a stranger on the street 'I will give you £100' that does not constitute a contract and the stranger wouldn't be able to force you to pay up. But if you were to offer to

give £100 if he wrote you a poem, and he agreed to do that, then that would be a legal contract. An offer, an agreement and a payment of some kind are the three key elements of a contract.

If I paid for it, I must own the copyright to it.

This is not necessarily so, no matter how much you paid. Going back to basics, if you write a book or create an original design for something (a better looking salad bowl, perhaps) then you immediately, without doing anything, have legal copyright on those things. That means if anyone copies them without your permission you can demand compensation. If an employee writes or designs something as part of his or her work for your business, again you (or your limited company) own the copyright. But if you get an outside agency to do the writing and designing, unless you have an agreement saying otherwise, then it will own the copyright. This principle also applies to work done for you by an advertising agency or website designer. Paying thousands for a new advert only to find that, when you switch agencies, you don't own the copyright to it, so that you are not free to reproduce it as you choose, can be a real shocker. To avoid this situation, ask your solicitor to draw up a contract for use with external suppliers that clearly states you hold the copyright on anything they produce for you.

Getting a patent costs a fortune and isn't worth the hassle.

The first part of this Stupid Factor may have some validity, but the second part certainly doesn't. If you develop an invention that is important to the success of your business (and it must be an invention, such as a product or process – you can't patent anything as vague as an idea or even a computer program, although this may be protected by copyright law), you should consider patenting it. Not least because you will only attract investors if your invention, which will be viewed as a strategic asset, cannot be copied with impunity by anyone else. Without a patent, you can guarantee that someone bigger than you will eventually use your own invention, if it takes off, to take away your customers, and there'll be nothing you can do about it.

To be eligible for a patent your invention must be original and its existence must not yet be public knowledge – so don't be too hasty putting out a press release or even telling potential investors, unless they sign a confidentiality agreement first. Filing a patent application costs nothing – just fill in the forms supplied by The Patent Office (**www.patent.gov.uk** – find out about trademarks and registering designs here, too). You then have up to a year to decide whether to proceed with the application; if you do, you need to fill in a couple more forms and pay fees totalling £200. As soon as you have filed your patent application, you are free to make your invention public. If your patent is eventually granted (i.e. the invention is deemed to be original and the sort of thing that can be patented), anyone copying it from this time can be taken to court.

Think this all sounds a bit too easy? You're right. Writing a patent – basically a description of an invention – is a skilled business. If it isn't done well then others may be able to break it – produce something that is effectively the same as your invention, but with a slight modification so that they aren't infringing your patent. You therefore need to consult with a chartered patent agent (you can find them in the Yellow Pages) who will say if you have a patentable invention and also write the patent for you. Using these people will, alas, cost you money, so that registering your patent may actually cost you anything from a thousand pounds to over ten thousand. You may also want to pay for the agent or The Patent Office's Search and Advisory Service to do a thorough search to make sure your invention is original before you spend money on the application. This will cost at least £500, though you could try doing this yourself. If your patent is granted, which can take between two-and-a-half and four-and-a-half years, it will last for 20 years, provided you pay a modest annual fee to renew it. Finally, a UK patent is only applicable in this country – you must make further applications for protection in other countries.

 ### If I tell someone something confidential about my business they aren't allowed to talk about it with anyone else.

As your business gets going, you may have to provide sensitive information to a whole host of people. For example, you might need to tell your PR agency about contracts you are about to win so it can plan a press campaign around them, or give a potential investor an insight into an industrial process you've developed but not yet patented. In both cases you might suppose that there is an assumption of confidentiality, and that obviously they must keep these things to themselves. And in the event of a dispute – such as the investor starting his or her own company in competition to you using your process – you might successfully make that argument in court. But you will make life much easier and more secure for yourself by getting people to sign a confidentiality agreement before you tell or show them anything sensitive. Also known as non-disclosure agreements (or even NDAs is you want to sound ultra cool), it's no big deal to get your solicitor to create one for you, and nobody honest should object so signing one. Interestingly, over the many years that I have been working with businesses, ranging from small start-ups to multi-billion dollar corporations, providing marketing and PR consultancy, I have never been asked to sign one of these. I must have an honest face, I suppose.

Solicitors

All but the simplest of start-ups will soon require the services of a solicitor, so it's worth lining one up early. Ask people in your business networks for personal recommendations, and then meet with several. This first contact is important – if they don't seem to understand your business or are not particularly interested in what you do, look elsewhere. Get them to explain how they operate, including how they charge. They should also readily hand out a checklist of things that the founder of a new business needs to consider. The solicitor you use must be able to make even complicated legal issues easy for you to understand, rather than making it all seem like a black art. In addition, you may need legal advice in a hurry if, for example, a sacking turns ugly or a contract negotiation gets sticky. That means you must be confident your solicitor will take your calls in an emergency or have meetings outside normal office hours. You should also take references from a solicitor's clients.

When might you use your carefully chosen lawyer? Anything you do relating to property – buying or even short-term leasing – will need one to get involved, checking and explaining the finer points of any agreements. He or she can also help on employment matters.

Lawyers commonly assist with drawing up contracts with suppliers and customers, along with franchise and confidentiality agreements. They can also advise on intellectual property and generally provide 'wise counsel', such as if you are made an offer that seems too good to be true and you're worried it could be a scam.

Lawyer's top tips

Being realistic, you won't always get third parties to sign a piece of paper every time something is agreed. So to support your case in the event of a dispute, whenever something has been agreed with a customer or supplier, such as in a meeting or telephone call, write him (or her) a letter summarising what was discussed. If he doesn't respond to say he disagrees with what you have written, then that could work to your advantage in court.

Solicitors generally charge on a time basis, so to keep your legal costs down you should try to use up as little of it as possible. An easy way to do that is to always be fully prepared for any meetings you have with them by bringing along all the paperwork that could conceivably be relevant. Also, always give them a complete picture of your situation from the outset, so that they can immediately give you the best possible advice.

Don't be afraid to complain to your solicitors or ask them to explain their charges. Indeed, they should always give a breakdown of their costs. You can also ask if they will work for a fixed fee, or at least provide an estimate. Even try appealing to the entrepreneur lurking in your lawyers, and see if they will do work on a speculative basis. For example, you might ask them to support a new development in your business by not charging a fee up front – but, of course, they should be amply rewarded when the venture eventually proves a success and they can finally submit their bill.

Make your lawyers, or any other professionals you employ, feel like part of the team by inviting them to social events, such as your launch party. And don't hesitate to tell them if you think they've done a good job – it could pay dividends when you need a favour.

A limited company has to have a qualified accountant looking after its books.

You will need an accountant to do your company's annual accounts and its tax return (and possibly your own tax return as well if you choose). Otherwise, you can handle your business's books as you see fit as long as they are up-to-date and accurate – perhaps by doing them yourself with the help of a bookkeeper. If you do this you will save yourself a heap of money compared with just sending off boxes of receipts and invoices to your accountant every month for him or her to sort out. It will also make you better informed and more in control of your company, which will compensate for the time that handling the books takes from your working day. Note: you must keep your accountancy records for at least five years in case the tax man wants to see them.

 ## Accountants are all the same, so it doesn't matter which one you hire as long as he's qualified and wears a suit.

The right accountant for your company needs to be more than just a competent number cruncher; he or she should also demonstrate an understanding of your business and its particular needs. Ideally, he or she will have experience working in your industry sector. The accountant should also have empathy with your business's ethos and culture – just like any other professional service providers you employ.

An accountant who acts more like a bookkeeper, and doesn't provide the innovative ideas and positive input you need to develop your business isn't much use to you. However, one who works with you to anticipate problems and find appropriate solutions is a valuable asset, and this is the kind you should take the trouble to find.

Accountants

Most start-ups are better off using an external accountant rather that hiring one full time. This avoids having an extra salary to pay, therefore keeping down the business's overheads.

The accountant should be chosen carefully because he (or she) can be an important part of your team, providing advice and acting in many ways like a mentor. He must also be able to gain the respect of your managers and co-owners, so that his advice gets taken on board. Recommendations from your network can steer you in the right direction when making your choice, but still use your own judgement about whether a particular accountant will be able to provide the attentive service your start-up needs and is also someone you can get on with. And talk to more than one before making a decision.

New businesses are generally better off using a smaller accountancy firm, because it is more likely to provide the personalised service they need and it will also be cheaper than using a big name. You should find an accountant who is happy to help set up your internal accounting systems by suggesting which processes to adopt and recommending a computerised accounts package that is compatible with their own systems. The accountant should provide advice on how you can use a bookkeeper to both keep you constantly informed about what's happening financially in your business and also to minimise your overall accountancy costs. He should also be willing to provide help with financial planning, if required.

There are many ways in which your accountant can save you money, including helping you and your business pay as little tax as possible. But this can only happen if you keep him informed about what you are doing – so talk to your accountant when you do anything financially significant, such as a large purchase or the sale of major capital equipment. It may be that you would be better off leasing rather than purchasing, or delaying the sale until the next accounting period.

Your accountant should also provide advice regarding Value

Added Tax (VAT). He can tell you if it's worth registering for VAT, which will mean you having to charge your customers VAT. If you are selling to consumers this will make your product more expensive, but business customers won't care because they'll simply claim back any VAT they pay. The big advantage of registering is that you will be able to claim back the VAT on anything you buy for your business; on the downside, you will have to complete a VAT return each year to HM Revenue & Customs. It's important to remember that once your turnover reaches a certain level (in the 2006 budget it was set at £61,000) you must register immediately, or risk heavy fines.

9

Money Monkey

As we've already seen, in business the numbers are all-important. You will have already taken a close look at the finances of your start-up when you put your business plan together. But that was something you could do at your own pace and to your own level of satisfaction. When your business is actually up and running, you will have to keep track of your accounts while at the same time running your business, and do it to a standard that will please the tax man and any investors. This is no easy matter, with a survey by Barclays Bank showing that up to a third of small business owners' time can be taken up by this sort of activity.

Beyond fulfilling your statutory obligations, you also need to keep constant track of your finances so that you can effectively manage and develop your start-up. Keeping a close eye on the money can make the difference between success and failure, and going bust simply because you aren't 'good with figures' is not much of an excuse. If numbers are a problem for you then take steps to deal with this from the start – go on a basic numeracy or mathematics course (also consider a bookkeeping or basic accounting course) and talk to your accountant about putting practical financial systems in place. Also, make full use of the financial technology that is now readily available to all businesses, which ranges from smart cash registers to easy-to-use business software. But whatever you do, don't ignore the numbers and simply hope your accountant can make sense of it all in a year's time.

If I'm selling, I must be making money.

 Don't take anything for granted with your business. Of course, in the planning stage you should have worked out prices to cover your costs and make a profit, but it's a different matter when you actually start trading. You will probably encounter costs you didn't anticipate or underestimated, which will eat into profit margins. These may be fixed costs, in which case the total volume of sales will be as important as the value of individual sales in helping you make a profit. Variable costs, such as the cost of components for a product you are manufacturing, may also be higher than expected, so that you may need to increase the price of each unit to make a profit (or source a cheaper supplier). It may be as simple as finding that the total cost of packing and shipping, if you are selling through a website, is higher than expected, so either charge more for P&P or find a cheaper carrier.

The point is that it is only by keeping a close eye on costs from the start that you can be sure that what you are doing is making money. A high volume of sales and a general feeling of being busy isn't enough to ensure you are generating a profit.

There's no point keeping constant track of the business's accounts. This will only tell me things I can't do anything about or that I won't understand.

Anything that involves you knowing less and relying more on blind faith is almost certainly going to be a Stupid Factor, and hiding from the accounts is no exception. Money – getting it, keeping it and spending it – is what every business is all about, and it is the thing you need to be most intimate with as you begin and grow your start-up. On a weekly, if not daily, basis you should know:

- what sales you have made and what expenses have been incurred
- your stock levels
- your gross profit and fixed costs, so you can quickly calculate net profit
- how much money your business has in the bank, in the tills and elsewhere
- the money others owe you (your customer debt – how much and for how long)

- what you owe others (your credit with suppliers and when this must be paid).

Keeping track of this much information may at first seem a daunting task, but by implementing just a few simple procedures and sticking to them it will soon become a straightforward, continuous process.

Staying on top of the books doesn't require you to have an MBA or employ a full-time company accountant; anyone can do it, and it can help out your business big time as it starts to take off. Most obviously, if you spot that sales are dropping you can find out why and then remedy the situation, before it harms your bottom line. Is a competitor taking business away from you? Do you need to adjust your prices or enhance your service?

If you see that your profit margin is shrinking, this tells you to look at the efficiency of your operation. Have supplier costs gone up, and so should you look for new suppliers? Are your salespeople discounting prices, and if so do they need more training so they can sell without having to do this?

Perhaps most importantly, by knowing what money is entering and leaving your business (i.e. your cashflow) you can predict when money will become tight, and make arrangements to handle this (see **Overtrading**, page 141) – possibly dodging bankruptcy in the process!

⚠ Shaving a few pence off costs here and there won't make much difference.

This Stupid Factor is similar to **If I'm selling, I must be making money** in as much as it relates to your business's profitability. However, here the problem stems more from arrogance, expedience and short sightedness, rather than blind faith and naivety.

There is a well-observed tendency for start-ups to be very free with their money in the early stages. Bedazzled by a wildly over-optimistic business plan which shows them making vast profits from day one, many entrepreneurs decide that keeping a close eye on both set-up and operating costs isn't worth the effort. This attitude is further reinforced by the big numbers that can be involved in starting a business. The cost of premises, for example, may be so high as to make all other costs seem negligible. And if you are lucky enough to secure generous outside investment for your project, the temptation to spend big can be almost irresistible.

However, even if things go as well as your business plan predicts, chances are your profit will be relatively small compared to your start-up and operational costs. This means that the difference between profit and loss could hinge on the costs you didn't bother to take the time to control. Suddenly, the ten per cent discount you neglected to haggle from suppliers, or the extra few grand you kicked into the transportation budget to get yourself a flashier motor, or your fondness for flying first class rather than economy on international sales trips, represents the profit you are failing to make. Quite apart from the aggro you will get from investors and your accountant, no profit means no money to re-invest in the business to make it grow. The difference between success and failure can easily hang on avoiding this Stupid Factor.

Controlling costs

'Every penny you spend is a penny less profit.' How you relate to that statement can have major implications for your start-up. Take it too literally and you could end up not spending enough on functions that are important to your business, such as marketing. Or you could make short-term savings that will cost you dearly in the future – such as hiring a salesperson because they are cheap rather than good, or not adequately insuring your premises, or neglecting to get vital professional advice. Balancing long-term costs against short-term savings is something every entrepreneur needs to be conscious of during the crucial early days of a business.

On the other hand, failing to see a direct link between your company's costs and its profits can also be bad news. It's easy to use the old saying 'You need to spend money to make money' to excuse your extravagancies.

One way to tackle this issue is to think about the time and effort involved in earning the money you are about to spend. Suddenly, devoting a couple of hours to finding a way to spend £1,000 less a month on shipping may seem like a great use of your time. But taking up a whole day phoning stationery suppliers to save a few quid on copier paper may not be worth it. The crucial thing is to take cost control seriously from day one, and be as smart about how you spend your money as how you make it.

The good news is that there are a number of simple cost-control mechanisms that any business can implement which quickly bring benefits. One is to allocate a budget for particular business activities. This should stimulate attempts to get maximum value from a limited resource, assuming the budget isn't set too high and a number of other steps are taken. These include the use of purchase order numbers (POs) to keep track of spending. This is a procedure whereby every order made by an employee has a PO associated with it. The cost of the order (or at least an estimate), the name of the employee placing the order, the details of the supplier and the expected delivery date should be recorded against the PO when it is issued by you or your purchasing manager. It should also be in your written terms and conditions for suppliers that their invoices will only be paid if they have a PO number associated with them. All this immediately helps you keep track of company spending. It also makes employees directly accountable for the purchases they make.

There should be a policy of obtaining competitive quotes for purchases over a certain value. Businesses typically require quotes from three different suppliers before spending more than a few hundred pounds, but you should be careful about putting a definite figure on the number of quotes. If you say three quotes, then employees will get three quotes, but for a high-value or strategic purchase it may be worth getting many more. This tendering process, in which multiple suppliers are asked to provide a price for supplying the same product or service, is also a chance to find the supplier likely to give the highest quality or the most generous payment terms, as well as the lowest price. Once again, the time you devote to this process should relate to the money you expect to save or the advantage you expect to gain by choosing the best supplier.

You should also educate your staff on the importance of cost control. The link between your business's costs and its profitability may be obvious to you, but that doesn't mean it will be to your employees. They may, for example, be buying first-class train tickets to see low-value clients or sales prospects, without realising that by doing so they are blowing any profit to be made from them. So don't be afraid to spell out the cost/profit connection. You might even include something about taking a responsibility for cost control in their job description or your business's staff manual.

You should also think carefully about what staff you really need, including the total number, the roles they will fill and their individual cost, and see if savings can be made here. The easiest saving is to only hire people you really need. For example, learning to type and use a PC (which almost anyone can do in a couple of weeks) may not only remove the need to hire yourself a PA, it may even save you time, as the act of delegating a task can often take longer than the task itself. Another trick is to not employ a dedicated receptionist to answer the telephone. Instead, make all employees responsible for answering the phone or use a voice processor or a 'virtual' telephone reception service to retain the human touch. These options can save time for you and your customers alike, as well as cutting your wage bill. Also, if a job doesn't require an expensive graduate to do it, then don't employ one. Having someone with a philosophy degree stacking pallets in the warehouse may well make tea breaks more stimulating, but if it's costing you extra money just take some Nietzsche to work instead.

A great place for start-ups to save cash is with their fixed overheads, as by definition these will be hardest to change once they are trading. Top of the list will be the cost of premises. Here it pays to be as flexible as possible in relation to type, specification, size, general location and geography. If it doesn't matter to your business that it's located in a corner suite in a swish, city centre office block in the South East of England, then don't make that a priority. As a matter of interest, potential investors will often be impressed by a start-up that has chosen somewhere cheap and cheerful to locate, as this indicates its directors are careful with the company's money.

Making capital purchases now will save us money in the long term – after all, we've got lots of cash/credit, so we may as well spend it.

This is a Stupid Factor that can afflict start-ups big and small: making big purchases when renting or leasing would be the lower-risk option. A typical example would be to buy shop premises – with the bank more than happy to give you a mortgage – rather than rent. Suddenly, you would have a valuable asset that increases in value rather than be chucking money into a black hole, so good idea, right? Maybe, but ask yourself whether you are in the business of running a shop or property speculation? Forcing a business to repay a big mortgage, rather than a modest rent, could wipe out its profit so that it has no money for expansion. It might be more rational to keep your property tycoon aspirations separate from your new business.

Alternatively, you may be a hi-tech start-up that's secured impressive first round financing – well done! With millions in the bank, the temptation to splash out on an office building or a big piece of equipment can be overwhelming. After all, your finance-winning business plan shows that half the new money won't be needed by the business for another nine months, and if things go as well as you secretly hope (rather than as you told the investors, when you were trying to appear conservative) you may not need it at all! But what if sales are slow to take off and you need to do more marketing or further product development? Suddenly you have no room to manoeuvre because all your spare cash (which was never really spare) is tied up in a capital purchase.

As it happens, almost anything you might want for a business, from cars to computers to desks, can be leased. Deciding what to buy and what to lease is often tricky, as you balance short-term cashflow implications against long-term costs. It is, therefore, important to take professional advice before deciding whether to lease or buy, rent or get a mortgage. For example, leasing may reduce your tax bill, which would offset some of the long-term costs of not buying, but it's only by talking to your accountant that you can be sure what's best for your business.

Overtrading

Most start-ups go out of business not because they fail to win customers and make a profit, but because they overtrade. In fact, ironically, a company that is apparently doing well with lots of sales may be more vulnerable than one that is scraping by.

Overtrading occurs when money is leaving the business quicker than it is coming in, so that there isn't enough cash to fund the business. For example, if your suppliers need paying in two weeks, but you won't get money from customers for 30 days, and there's nothing in your business's bank account, then you are overtrading. For a shop, it can occur if you purchase too much stock in one go. In the case of a builder, it could be buying building materials and hiring staff for a big contract without either enough money in the bank or a sizable deposit from the customer. An obvious way for any company to avoid overtrading is to get the most generous possible payment terms from suppliers, while giving customers as little time as possible to pay you.

You might also get credit facilities in place in case you inadvertently overtrade (perhaps because you weren't keeping close track of your accounts). Examples would be an overdraft facility with the bank or credit cards you can make balance transfers from. Such instant credit can be expensive in the longer term, and so should only be used to handle short-term difficulties. For long-term financing of your business, to fund growth for example, see **Ways to finance your start-up,** page 87.

If you find you have overtraded, the first thing to do is to get on the phone to suppliers and customers alike. Ask the former to give you as much leeway as possible in paying their bills, and the latter to pay their invoices ASAP. The worst strategy is to do nothing and just hope things will turn out okay.

10

Hire 'em and Fire 'em

For many entrepreneurs, taking on their first employees can be a significant moment. Not only does it mean their business idea is finally turning into a business reality, but it also forces them to take on responsibilities they may be totally unfamiliar with. Hiring, managing, paying and possibly firing people can all seem like seriously scary stuff, especially with the blizzard of new employment laws that constantly blow out of Brussels. But taking on staff can also be an exciting and rewarding experience – if you avoid the many Stupid Factors that lay in wait for you here.

The fact that you are suddenly dealing with people, rather than business models, spreadsheets and inanimate assets, can be a shock to the system. It can see you doing things you would never do under normal circumstances – acting on impulse, ignoring common sense and disregarding good business practice. What you need to do is treat taking on and managing staff as you would any business activity – plan ahead, don't cut corners, take advice and base your decisions on what is good for the start-up, not your ego. Get it right, and you will be getting your new venture off to a brilliant start; get it wrong and the venture could very soon fail.

 There's no point wasting a lot of time on the recruitment of staff: a trained monkey could do this job.

In reality, there are very few jobs that absolutely anyone can do. Even if you do have such positions, there will always be some people better suited to doing them than others. If you are in any doubt about that, try writing as detailed a description as you can of what an anyone-can-do-it job entails, along with the skills and knowledge that will be required. Then add the more general qualities you would want from an employee, such as reliability, punctuality and honesty. It will show that even the most mundane job can be surprisingly demanding, and that you might not want to hire just anyone to do it. This exercise should also indicate how you will need to manage such staff.

 Okay, perhaps some people would be better at this job than others, but the effort required to find and supervise these perfect employees would never be worth it. If staff are no good or can't manage themselves I'll just sack them and get new ones.

The trouble with this employment philosophy is that it ignores the cost of hiring and firing – which can soon add up to a profit-threatening sum if you have a high turnover of staff. First there's the expense of finding employees, including any advertising and employment agency fees; then there's the administrative overhead of putting them on the payroll; and specific costs, such as providing a uniform and training. And don't forget the cost of having someone do a job incorrectly or unproductively because they are unsuited or aren't adequately supervised. As for getting rid of employees, unless you want to risk being taken to an Industrial Tribunal (and believe me, you don't) you can't simply sack them with immediate effect without very good reason. Even if they have only been with you for a very short time, you will at least have to give them one week's notice or provide pay in lieu along with any accrued holiday pay. Worse still, you may decide that getting rid of an unsuitable employee and finding someone new isn't worth the hassle, so that your business is suffering from their unsuitability for years to come.

It should now be obvious to you that spending time on hiring the right people from the start, and managing them so that they both do a good job and stay with your company, makes solid business sense. And that this applies whether they are high-powered graduates or school leavers.

I know the sort of managers I want to hire, and I'll recognise them when I see them.

Thinking in terms of a general type of person you want to hire is probably one of the easiest traps to fall into when hiring staff at a senior level. With that attitude you'll probably end up hiring people just like you – an army of Mini-mes to help run your empire. But Mini-mes may not be the best option, no matter how great you think you are.

When hiring managers, you should instead think in terms of (a) the particular role that needs filling and (b) building an effective team to run the company. The first point means letting the job role determine the person you take on, rather than starting with the sort of person you want to hire (see below). The second point means you should try to take on managers with complementary strengths rather than the same skills, experience and personality. In that way you can acquire in-house expertise across all the business functions with a team that can handle all kinds of challenges. If, however, everyone is just like you (for example, you only hire super-assertive, non-graduate salespeople like yourself) then there will inevitably be skill gaps, and situations that can't be tackled because there is no one with strategic vision or coolness under pressure or fluency in Japanese.

Hiring staff: first principles

First consider what exactly you'll want a new employee to do. This may seem self-evident, but a surprising number of people are employed simply on a general notion of needing more people or, worse still, on the deeply flawed principle that 'there's always room in my organisation for a good man'. A useful exercise would be for you to spend a day doing the job that you think needs a new employee. As well as confirming that there really is a job that needs doing, this will help you when it comes to the first critical step in hiring new staff: role profiling. This means writing a detailed description of what the job entails, followed in turn by a description of what the employee must be able to do in order to perform the job effectively.

An important purpose of role profiling is to stop you becoming unnecessarily focused on qualifications and, worse still, thinking in terms of what a new member of staff should be like rather than what they can do. This approach, where you start with the person you want rather than the position you need to fill, will unnecessarily limit your employee options – which given the current shortage of skilled (and even unskilled) workers could seriously harm your business. For example, you may want a male graduate in his mid-twenties who plays team sports to be your first salesperson, but a non-graduate, non-sporty woman in her forties, with bags of relevant experience, could be just as good. In other words, don't let empty prejudices influence your employment decisions.

The principle of spreading your employment net as wide as possible should follow through into where you look for applicants. This means briefing your recruitment agency, if you are using one, in such a way that they don't overlook potentially suitable candidates because they, too, are thinking in terms of the kind of person you want or are using some arbitrary selection criteria, such as a minimum number of GCSEs obtained. And if you are advertising for candidates, pick media that will provide you with the largest number of suitable respondents rather than, say, the largest number of people you think you'd enjoy having a pint with.

Likewise, the application form you use should help the applicant present evidence that they can do the job well, not what kind of person they are. So don't ask irrelevant questions, such as 'What are your interests?' which is very unlikely to tell you anything useful. When assessing the applications you should, therefore, be matching up experience and abilities with your role profile, which will make choosing candidates for interview a rational process rather than so much guesswork.

The interview itself is a chance for applicants to provide further evidence that they can do the job. That means getting them to talk in specific terms about what they can do. Do not accept, and certainly don't encourage, general statements in this area from interviewees – it is for you to make the generalisations, not them. Similarly, if you need to know if someone has specific technical knowledge, then ask specific questions in that area; don't assume they have the necessary knowledge. One thing, in particular, to look out for with interviews is to not be unduly influenced by your first impressions. Studies have clearly shown that interviewers will often let a first impression colour how they interpret what the candidate subsequently says. The rule is to listen to what candidates are actually saying, and ignore such irrelevances as their choice of business suit, or how smiley they were when they walked into the room.

I don't want to give the impression that employing people is simply a procedural exercise: you crank a handle and out pops the perfect employee. Anything that involves 'people' rather than 'things' is bound to be more complicated than that, so you must use common sense when making your final selection. Just because someone gets a tick in all the boxes doesn't mean they will be the right person for your start-up. In particular, if a suitably qualified individual clearly doesn't understand or empathise with the aims of your business, they are unlikely to make a good employee. Of course, you need to clearly and succinctly put across to your candidates what your business is about – in the job ad, on the application form and at the interview – in order to determine their understanding and empathy. Writing a short, simple mission or vision statement can be a useful starting point to help you do this. The Disney Corporation's is supposedly 'To make people happy', which is something everyone in the company can use to guide them in their day-to-day work – or decide if they even want a job there. (You can count me out!)

Another instance of where you could be tempted to go against common sense is to hire someone who isn't enthusiastic about working for you. Yes, it may sound crazy but companies often employ people who have shown every indication of not being keen. Examples I have come across include hiring people who initially turned down a job because it wasn't interesting enough; were belligerent and dismissive at the interview; made unreasonable demands for greater pay and benefits; wanted a post other than the one they'd applied for; didn't turn up for an agreed trial work day. In none of these instances did things turn out well with the new employee, which is no surprise as you can't expect a person to magically change the day they start a new job: if they are initially unenthusiastic they'll stay that way.

Likewise, if an otherwise perfect candidate currently lacks a fundamental ability don't kid yourself you can help him or her acquire it overnight. That's not to say specific skill gaps, such as the use of a particular piece of office software, can't be filled pretty easily. But with something more basic, such as a new salesperson's ability to sell, you shouldn't even consider letting someone pick this up on the job. Big corporations are often happy to wait a few months for an employee to become fully productive; start-ups can rarely afford such a luxury. So if someone doesn't immediately have what it really takes to do the job at hand, look elsewhere, even if that will cost you extra time and money in the short term. After all, why else did you do all that role profiling in the first place?

Employing people is a scary business these days, so I'll just hire friends and family.

On the face of it, this may not seem such a bad idea. After all, you would be employing people you know and trust, and who are likely to show as much commitment to the business as yourself. Indeed, for an entrepreneur with an inexhaustible supply of talented friends and hardworking family to call upon, it could be hard to fault such an employment strategy. However, it is worth highlighting its potential weakness: by only taking on friends and family, you are limiting your options and possibly making do with second best. Your brother, for example, may be a reasonable salesman, but wouldn't it be better to find a very good salesperson? And having hired a friend to a key position, what if it turns out they aren't up to the job? You then have to make the tough choice between making the right business decision (i.e. dismissing the person) and losing a friend, or harming your business (i.e. letting your chum retain a job he or she can't do well) and keeping the friendship.

 ## I'll make life very easy for myself and only hire people on a self-employed basis.

This can make life easier... but as always there's a flip side. With self-employed contractors you don't have the hassle of paying their tax or, more significantly, the expense of paying National Insurance Contributions. Plus, if you don't need them anymore you just stop using them, with no need to worry about being taken to an Industrial Tribunal for unfair dismissal.

But just because people say they're a self-employed contractor, and you regard them as self-employed, that doesn't mean that Her Majesty's Revenue & Customs (HMRC) will regard them as self-employed. The taxman will judge whether someone is employed or self-employed according to 'the terms, condition and facts' of their employment. That means applying a number of tests:

- Does the person have to do the work himself or herself?
- Can you tell the person at any time what to do, where to carry out the work or when and how to do it?
- Does the person work a set amount of hours?
- Can you move the person from task to task?

- Is the person paid by the hour, week, or month?
- Can the person get overtime pay or bonus payment?

Answer yes to any of the above and the taxman may say the person is an employee. However, if you answer yes to any of the following, the HMRC will probably judge he or she as self-employed.

- Can the person hire someone else to do the work or engage helpers at their own expense?
- Does the person risk their own money?
- Does the person provide the main items of equipment needed to do their job, not just the small tools many employees provide for themselves?
- Did the person agree to do the job for a fixed price, regardless of how long the job may take?
- Can the person decide what work to do, how and when to do the work and where to provide the services?
- Does the person regularly work for a number of different people?
- Does the person have to correct unsatisfactory work in his or her own time and at their own expense?

Note that there are certain situations and particular industries where different rules apply, so if you are in any doubt about someone's status, take professional advice or visit the HMRC's website (**www.hmrc. gov.uk**) for the latest guidelines.

'So what?' you may say. *'If the taxman decides they are really employees, I'll just say I'm sorry and put them on the pay roll.'* Except that you will have been giving people what you considered gross payments, leaving it for them to pay any tax and National Insurance. The HMRC, though, will consider them net payments and demand that you pay the corresponding tax and National Insurance. That's right, you will pay this, not the employees, who now discover that they've effectively had a pay rise. Suddenly, this cheap and easy staffing option could prove rather expensive.

Discrimination

This is the area of employment law that you are most likely to fall foul of, but where trouble can be easily avoided by applying a little common sense. Discrimination legislation affects both the recruitment and the management of your staff. These laws cannot make you employ or prevent you from sacking whomever you please, but they can impose financial penalties, ranging from the relatively minor to the totally crippling. So if you have deep pockets you can ignore this section, otherwise read on to learn how to save yourself thousands.

Job applicants and employees are entitled to take a business that they believe has discriminated against them to an Industrial Tribunal (this is similar to a magistrates court, with no jury) at no cost to themselves (although they will have to pay for any legal counsel they choose to hire). You will have the expense of hiring legal counsel (unless you feel you can fight the action yourself), plus any fines which are imposed if you lose. Ignoring someone taking you to a Tribunal is not an option, as the case will simply be found against you in your absence.

It is illegal to discriminate against people on the basis of race, sex, religion, sexual orientation, disability or age. That means you cannot decline to hire someone because of any one of these factors, and you cannot treat one employee any differently to the rest because of these. (Some exceptions exist regarding gender, and disability can be an allowable factor if it represents a valid health and safety issue, but in either case you should seek expert advice before doing anything that could be viewed as discriminatory.)

Discrimination itself can be broken down into two forms: direct and indirect. Direct is the sort of blatant discrimination that you probably know instinctively not to do, such as placing an advertisement saying 'Wanted: attractive, young female bar staff' or 'Italian chef required for new restaurant'. In the workplace, if you were to refuse a request to promote someone on the basis that he or she is 'too old' that would also be direct discrimination.

Indirect discrimination is when you take actions that have the ultimate effect of discriminating against a particular group, even if they are not acts of discrimination in themselves. An example would be to only advertise positions in publications or on websites that will be viewed mostly by men. And when it comes to applicants, employees or even customers with a disability, if you fail to make 'reasonable adjustments' for them, perhaps by enabling wheelchair access or supplying a suitable computer keyboard, you could also get into trouble.

An easy first step to avoid accusations of discrimination when recruiting is to not include unnecessary questions on your application forms, such as those regarding age, marital status or hobbies. Likewise, if something isn't strictly necessary to do the job, such as having a particular qualification, then don't mention it in your advertisements. Note that using an employment agency that discriminates against applicants doesn't reduce your responsibility: your business will still be considered to have done the discriminating.

The big challenge for you as an employer will be to prove that discrimination was not a factor in your decision making should a dispute arise with a job applicant or employee. The key to doing this is to keep adequate records of your dealings with applicants and employees. Get into the habit of making notes in a day book or diary about such interactions – these needn't be mini-essays, just something to indicate what was said or done. But be warned, only ever write down or put in an email things that you wouldn't mind being seen in court. Scribbling a note during an interview that you think an applicant is 'totally gay' or similar won't do you any favours with the members of the Tribunal, even if it was done in jest.

It's worth noting that you are able to lay off employees without giving a reason within two years of taking them on, as long as you give them the notice required by their employment contract. However, if the person you get rid of believes you did so because you were discriminating against them on the basis of sex, age, etc, then things won't be so simple and you could end up at a Tribunal having to explain why you had to let them go.

Employment contracts are more trouble than they are worth.

In all the excitement of taking on your first employees, it can be very easy to overlook something as tedious as contracts. After all, anything of a legal nature is likely to (a) be boring and (b) cost your company money (solicitor's fees – who needs 'em!). And anyway, it was all very clear at the job interview what you expected of your new employee, and what they would be getting from you. Let's face it, once you start setting every little thing in stone with a contract it is as likely to get you into trouble as keep you out of it. Best keep things flexible and informal, yes?

In reality, once someone has been offered a job, and they have accepted that offer, there is a contract in place whether you like it or not, even if only a verbal one. The contract will be based on whatever terms and conditions were agreed between yourself and the employee. In addition, custom and practice in your business could also be taken to form part of this contract, as there is nothing in writing to state otherwise.

What's more, having nothing in writing (beyond a written statement of employment particulars, which is a legal obligation) will inevitably lead to misunderstandings and disagreements in the future, as each party struggles to remember what was agreed. This can easily result in an employer-employee relationship turning sour completely unnecessarily, so have whatever was agreed between your business and a new employee written down in a contract as soon as possible – don't put this off.

In fact, a well written contract can actually enhance relations with your employees. This is done by using it to clearly define what you expect from them, which allows you to manage and fairly assess their performance. Also, by clearly stating in the contract what procedures an employee should follow if they have a grievance, you can avoid petty upsets turning into full-scale disputes. The contract can even increase employee flexibility, for example by specifically stating that working hours and employment location are not fixed, or that there will be no overtime or time off in lieu for working unsocial hours. And when an employee leaves your company, having a well-written contract that defines notice period, holiday pay entitlement and the like can make the parting sweet sorrow, rather than bitter acrimony.

Having hopefully convinced you that employment contracts are a good idea (and not to be avoided out of expediency), you should talk to your solicitor or HR consultant about having a standard contract drawn up. You should also talk to them if you need to make amendments to this for a particular employee you are taking on. See Appendix 2 for an example employment contract.

Employees don't need to be told not to use the Internet at work for private purposes – they should know that already.

Blame the hippy drug culture of the Sixties if you will, but these days the boundary between what is considered acceptable and unacceptable behaviour for employees is very fuzzy. Most people would agree that shooting your colleagues with an AK47 is a dismissible offence (though God knows, we've all been tempted), but using the telephone or the Internet to book cinema tickets during a lunch break may be okay. These and many other issues, which aren't suitable for inclusion in an employment contract, should therefore be covered in a staff handbook. Carefully written, this document can clearly state company policy in numerous grey areas.

As well as aiding good employee relations, a handbook can be very useful in the event of a dispute with a member of staff. For example, if you find employees spend a lot of their time downloading images from a pornographic website onto their office computer, you are in a better position legally to reprimand or even dismiss them if this matter is covered in the handbook. See Appendix 2 for ideas on what else to include. The great thing about an employee handbook is that it can easily evolve, with bits added or amended over time as new issues crop up. After all, imagine using one from the 1950s to manage staff – misuse of typewriter ribbons was probably the hot issue of the day.

Managing staff: dos and don'ts

'Your employees are your greatest asset' may not be a terribly original sentiment, but that doesn't make it any less true. Yet time and again start-ups seem to go out of their way to neglect this asset, then wonder why they have poor productivity and high staff turnover. The biggest mistake that many employers make is to believe that money is the most important motivator for their employees, when numerous studies have shown this is not the case. An enjoyable working environment, the company of their colleagues, job satisfaction, an appropriate work load, the right level of stress, a sense of achievement and recognition for a job well done can all be much more important in both motivating and retaining staff. The bottom line is that good management of your staff can have a massive positive effect on how your business develops.

Specifically, imagine a start-up where all the employees care about doing a good job and seeing their company succeed. Now imagine an otherwise identical one where none of the employees care about anything except making it to the end of the working day and going home. Which firm would you invest in? Making your employees care is a big part of what good management is

all about, and what follows are pointers to help you achieve that goal. Even if you have no experience at all of managing others, by keeping these points in mind you stand a good chance of seeing a decent return on the investment you make in your number one asset. If they care, everyone wins.

DOs:

➔ **Do be honest with your employees.** It can be tempting to make something up when an employee asks awkward questions (e.g. *'Why can't I have a raise?'*). But you will invariably get caught out by this in the future, undermining the respect and loyalty of your staff. However, dishonesty needn't involve actually lying to your employees. Giving them unrealistic expectations about the business and the job they will be doing can be equally damaging, whereas being truthful can only work to everyone's advantage. This philosophy particularly applies to an employee's first days in a job. The temptation is to give him or her an easy ride, with a light workload, easier hours and lots of 'treats' (such as free lunches and a few trips to the pub). All this does is set up a false impression of what life will really be like in their new job, and when the honeymoon is over a few weeks down the line, resentments can set in which take a long time to go away. However, if employees are working hard from day one, then both you and they will soon know if this is a job they can handle. It's better to have staff resign after the first week than after three months.

→ **Do have a proper induction for new employees.** Personal story: I turned up for my first day in the PR department of a high-powered marketing agency in London only to find no one from the department there to greet me. Worse still, there was no desk, no chair and no computer waiting for me. Eventually, in the afternoon, some colleagues did turn up and a few days later I even got a desk. At no point was there any kind of formal introduction to the company or an explanation of systems and procedures, much less any training on how to use the Apple Macintosh computer that eventually landed on my desk (I'd only used PCs before). Less than a week into my new job, I'd decided that this was a bad move and considered resigning on the spot. Worse still, the bad impression I'd gained of my new employer at the start stayed with me for the rest of my time there. Result: for the sake a little planning and consideration, the agency had to contend with a malcontent employee for two years. Moral: whatever you do, an employee's first days in a new job will be very lonely and bewildering, but at least do what you can to make them tolerable. Along with telling him or her where the toilets are and how to make an expenses claim, you might consider assigning someone the task of being the newbie's mate for the first week. (Being considerate to new employees isn't intended to contradict previous comments

→ → →

about giving them a realistic workload from the start. Most people are keen to get stuck into a new job as soon as possible, and feel frustrated if there isn't much for them to do.)

➜ **Do actively manage your company culture.** This means deciding what kind of place you want your business to be, then thinking of ways to actually make it so. If you need all your employees to work as a close team then think of ways to develop a team spirit, perhaps with an office football team. Want a culture of honesty, openness and personal responsibility? Then why not post everyone's salary on the intranet.

➜ **Do make use of the probationary period.** Having chosen to include this in your employment contracts – with perhaps just a week's notice required by either party to terminate employment within the first three to six months – don't be afraid to use it. If it is obvious things aren't working out with an employee, perhaps because he or she doesn't have the skills and experience claimed or doesn't fit in with the company culture, then saying goodbye early on will prove best for both of you. As previously stated, it is unrealistic to expect an employee to change overnight into something they're not (e.g. a brilliant salesperson or an innovative technical director).

Prof Birchall says:

➜ **Do collect ideas from the coal face** - from the people doing the work on the shop floor. I know of one major corporation that researched the source of innovation within the company and discovered that, over the years, all its best ideas had come from just five employees in relatively lowly positions. Incremental innovation, in particular, comes from the rank and file employee. It is important, therefore, to create a listening environment – and don't think a suggestion box is all you need. Instead, engage with your employees directly to discover the ideas they may have for your business.

DON'Ts:

➜ **Don't be a stranger to your employees**. Talking to your staff and getting to know them as individuals is one of the most important things you can do as an employer. So no matter how busy you get, you must schedule plenty of time for being around your employees. Apart from anything else, this is the only way you will really know what's going on in your business. It's also the only way you can effectively manage and lead your workforce – emails and memos pinned to the notice board just can't compete with a chat over a cup of coffee for communicating your vision for the business. Also, your employees can often be your greatest source of good ideas – greater even than your fellow managers and investors. This means talking to them can actually save you time and money in the long run.

➜ **Don't tell people what to do.** I'm indebted to business consultant Peter Hunter for this insight. It's a fact that employees resent being told what to do, with the result that they often end up doing the opposite of what you originally wanted them to do. But it's also true that most employees want to do a good job, and are more than capable of doing so given the opportunity. So try as much as possible to get your employees to figure out what needs doing and the best way to do it. The bonus of this approach is that the very act of figuring things out for themselves will improve the quality of your staff, as they learn to be problem solvers rather than problem makers. They will also be much more likely to care.

➜ **Don't use 'employee empowerment' as an excuse not to manage staff.** Getting employees to think for themselves and take responsibility for their actions shouldn't be used as a way to dodge your responsibilities. Staff still need to be managed and taken care of. Also, there will always be decisions that only you can make, and your business will become paralysed if you avoid making these by passing an unrealistic degree of responsibility onto your employees. Everyone in the business (including you) needs to be clear about where their responsibilities end and yours begin, and feel confident that you will pick up those responsibilities when required. There should also be regular employee performance reviews and systems for holding individuals directly accountable for their actions (an example being the use of purchase order numbers, see page 137). If you don't like the idea of having to do all this then think twice about becoming an employer.

→ **Don't avoid putting employees under any stress**. At work, a little stress can be a good thing, as long as an employee feels they have control over their situation. A job with no stress, however, can be a very dull and depressing thing. Some people can handle more stress than others, and you should become sensitive to this amongst your staff. Personally, I only work well with lots of pressure and a constant sense of crises – some of your employees may well be the same, and you should capitalise on this. When the going gets tough...

HR is just a waste of money, especially for small companies. It's certainly not worth paying anyone to do it.

HR – Human Resources – is not a luxury that's only for big businesses. If you have employees, then HR is something you will have to do whether you like it or not. Employment contracts, terms and conditions, employee benefits, hiring and firing are all things that will need to be done, and therefore take up your time and probably the time of your senior managers. What's more, there's no avoiding the fact that employment is a complicated area, governed by legislation that's changing all the time. Just keeping on top of it can take up a not-inconsiderable amount of your precious time each month. And not keeping up with current employment law could cost you dearly if you are taken to an Industrial Tribunal. So it makes both practical and financial sense to look for help from people whose job it is to know all about this subject.

Unless you expect to quickly have a 100+ employees, employing a HR manager probably isn't worth the expense. But using a HR service provider could prove very cost effective. This external HR can draw up your standard employment contracts and help whenever you get involved in an area you don't feel confident with, such as sacking people or reducing staff turnover. If you have five or more employees you are legally obliged to set up a stakeholder pension scheme for them, and again you may want to talk to the HR (or your Independent Financial Advisor).

Leadership in new companies

Once you start your business you aren't simply an employee anymore and nobody expects you to act like one, especially your employees. That doesn't mean you should become a tyrannical dictator; instead, take responsibility for your business and try to inspire your staff to do the best they can. Also, a boss should always appear confident and in control – nobody appreciates being led by a wet lettuce.

Prof Birchall says:

A big part of successful leadership is formulating strategy for a changing world. Equally vital is being able to communicate that vision – succinctly putting across what your business is about. An inability to do this can be a major barrier to success, making it difficult to hire the best talent or convince other businesses that your new product can really help them. But you need to remember that the biggest part of communicating is listening, not telling.

As a leader you must look at how well you project yourself, particularly to important parties such as potential investors. These people are as much interested in the quality of the people involved in a start-up as anything else and will be asking themselves, *'Do these managers have the personality, skill and competences to take this business forward?'*

If you recognise that your ability to project yourself is somewhat lacking, don't despair - the ability to 'work the crowd' can be developed by anyone. The critical thing is to identify any weaknesses you have as a leader and to work on these.

11

The Long, Hard Sell

Selling is what being in business is all about. But in the excitement of setting up a new business (which is generally all about spending money rather than making it), it's very easy to lose sight of this. The result is that after you've moved into your premises, hired all your staff, bought lots of equipment and stock, then finally opened your doors for business, you suddenly find you haven't really planned how you will actually sell your product or service.

How does this happen? Perhaps it just seems self-evident how you will sell – you have a shop, so people will simply walk in. Or maybe you assumed that, after the hard work of finding finance for your business and developing your product, actually selling it would be relatively trivial – something to be sorted out once you are up and running, using whatever start-up capital you happened to have left.

In reality, marketing (a term which includes selling) your product or service should be one of the first things you think about. In your business plan it should be dealt with in very specific terms, and you must keep it front of mind at all times. Marketing, in fact, should influence all your key decisions, from product development to the design of your company logo.

I'm in no hurry to start selling. The longer I have to develop this product/service, the better.

This Stupid Factor particularly afflicts hi-tech start-ups, where their technology-minded founders are afraid to leave the development 'comfort zone' and get into the nitty-gritty of marketing and selling. In fact, selling is something you should be doing as soon as possible – thinking of it as an activity which follows on sequentially from development wastes both time and money. Imagine spending two years developing your product to your satisfaction only to discover, when you finally start selling, that it doesn't adequately match what your customers want to buy. Like it or not, you'd then be forced to do even more development. Also, you shouldn't underestimate the time it takes to develop your sales channel (that is, the means by which you will reach your market). As a former senior manager at Apple Computers told me, this can take as long as the actual product development.

As a bonus, by integrating selling with your development activity, you should avoid having to guess if your product or service is ready to go on the market. Instead, your customers will, by placing advanced orders or providing letters of intent, be telling you when it is ready. You will still need to make a decision about whether a product is ready to be actually sold – it's no use having all the features your customers want written on the box if the gizmo inside doesn't work. But that decision should be based on technical and business considerations, not your fear of moving out of the lab and into the real world.

This thing is so damn good it will sell itself.

Nothing is good enough to sell itself. There are innumerable examples of great products and services that should have sold well but didn't, while their inferior rivals succeeded. A great example is Sony's Betamax video format which was beaten in the consumer market by JVC's inferior VHS (with the technical superiority of Betamax being proven by its near-universal adoption for professional video use). Conversely, there's Microsoft's office software, which is now all conquering despite having no great superiority over rival offerings when it was first introduced. It wasn't damn good, but it did sell.

But how can a great product fail? Firstly, spending nearly all your time developing, by your estimation, the perfect product or service and very little time finding out what customers really want (and how much they are prepared to pay!) is unlikely to lead to success. There should never be a feeling of isolating yourself from your customers – instead, you should be talking to them all the time, especially during the development phase.

And assuming you do have the perfect offering for your market, how will customers know that? If they don't perceive the quality and value of what you are selling – through adequate marketing communications, possibly well in advance of actually 'going to market' – then there is no point making it better than anything anyone else is selling. Furthermore, if you haven't organised adequate distribution so that customers can easily get hold of what you're selling, its quality will, again, be irrelevant.

The point is that having the perfect offering doesn't remove the need to put as much effort into marketing as everyone else in your marketplace. You will still need to think about sales staff, brochures, advertisements, a PR campaign, a website, hiring a distribution manager and all the rest. Sorry, but that's just the way it is.

⚠ Stack it high and sell it cheap – that's how I'll win a share of the market.

At the heart of this Stupid Factor is the belief that price can be used as your main sales and marketing tool. By keeping prices low, the thinking goes, you can beat bigger, established competitors without having to invest heavily in marketing, a more innovative offering or, in retail, a shop in a prime high street location. This is rarely the case, though.

The idea that price is all-important may, in part, stem from the old economics class law that sales will increase in a predictable manner as you lower the price of something. However, it also goes on to say that as you reduce your price you are reducing your profit margin, so that eventually you'll reach a point where reducing the price to increase sales will not result in your making any more money. There is, therefore, an optimum price which balances sales volume and profit margin, and there will be little point going much below this. In other words, there's a limit to which you can sensibly reduce prices to win market share.

In any case, many people nowadays have difficulty accepting the basic premise of this 'law', namely that there is a direct link between price and sales volume. Instinctively, they understand that price is just one part of the equation that dictates how well something sells. Availability, convenience, style, perceived quality and brand image are also important. You may even find that selling at little more than cost (i.e. sacrificing total profit by setting prices at just above what it cost you to purchase or manufacture a product) will not increase your sales if price is not the primary concern of your customers.

⚠ I've had the glossy brochures printed, so that's the marketing over and done with.

Anyone who says this is probably confused about what marketing is (see next page), which leads to it being seen as a trivial activity that brings minimal benefit to the business. Instead, marketing should be thought of as a thread running throughout the business, and as much a management mindset as any particular activity.

A low view of marketing often results in a company being overly sales-led, with too much of its resources going into the establishment and support of a sales team. This then functions as an independent entity in the business, divorced from such important activities as product development and customer service, which can soon lead to problems and missed opportunities.

One immediate negative consequence of this sales-led approach is that other marketing activities – PR, advertising, customer newsletters, market research and the like – are seen as luxury items, which make only a minimal contribution to the business's bottom line. In fact, they can often massively improve the effectiveness of the sales team, and hence of the marketing campaign as a whole, at a relatively modest cost. They can even result in your future customers mainly coming to you – rather than you having to go to them through an expensive sales team.

Marketing defined

Marketing is: selling customers what they want, the way they want it. However, it is more commonly seen the other way around – getting customers to buy what you're selling, the way you've chosen to sell it. The difference between these two approaches may seem pretty academic if they have the same end result – customers buying what you're selling. But it can quickly prove critical when you find the reverse is true – nobody seems to want what you've got to sell.

Using the selling-customers-what-they-want definition means seeing marketing as something that should pervade every aspect of your business. It may even be useful to view marketing as your principle business activity, and that everything else you do is in support of this. By now, you should have a clear idea of who your principal customers are, and it is their needs and desires that must dictate product development, pricing, distribution and after-sales service.

We all know the term 'marketing' also refers to the range of things you can do to actually sell, or at least raise awareness of, your product or service. These are usually seen as ways of persuading as many customers as possible to buy what you're selling. But if we are serious about adopting a selling-what-they-want attitude, we must instead see these marketing tools as informing a select group of customers (i.e. your target market) that what you're selling is what they already want to buy, even if they haven't quite realised that yet. If that strikes you as an unnecessarily twisted and obscure, then so be it. But at least try to keep an open mind to the possibility that your marketing activity can do more than just say, 'This is what I'm selling: this is what it does, this is what it costs, please buy it.'

The marketing mix

Way back when you were writing your business plan, I asked you to think in as much detail as possible about your market and to identify the sectors of it where you expected to dominate. You should also have already thought about how you will market your business to these sectors. Now is the time to look in even greater detail at this and examine the marketing tools at your disposal.

A general principle that is applied in marketing is to use a range of activities to communicate with your customers, or as the marketing professionals say, to use the 'marketing mix'. There are several reasons for taking this approach. Most obviously, you can't rely on a single medium, such as an advertisement in a local newspaper or trade magazine, reaching all your potential customers. Secondly, not everyone responds well to a particular marketing approach, with some people being effectively blind to online advertising or direct mail, for example. Thirdly, there is a cumulative effect as customers get exposed to your business in various ways. If they see your advertisement they may find it interesting but aren't motivated to act. But if they subsequently read about your product or service in a magazine article, they may become even more interested, and when a piece of direct mail arrives with a special offer it could be the final push they need to purchase.

For maximum impact you should carefully co-ordinate your marketing activities. That means planning ahead and having an actual marketing campaign, rather than a whole load of random activities taking place in isolation. So if, for example, you choose to sponsor a local sports team next season, that would be the best time for your advertising and PR activity to kick in, acting in support of the sponsorship and giving you maximum benefit from it. When customers read about your business in the newspaper, hear its advert on the radio, and then see its name in six-feet-high letters at the sports ground then there is a real danger they will actually buy what you're selling – so you should have trained salespeople ready to take their telephone calls.

To get the most from the marketing mix, you should be saying essentially the same thing with each activity. If your advertising contradicts your PR or direct mail, for example, your customers will be confused, which is something to be avoided. So your first step with any marketing campaign must be to determine what your core messages are: what are the three or four things that you want to communicate to your customers which are most likely to motivate them to make a purchase? These messages will usually be the key features of what you're selling along with, critically, the benefits these bring to the customer. It is important to spend some time writing down these individual messages, so that they can then be adapted for each marketing activity. For example, if your core message is 'We deliver within 24 hours', you may well want to say exactly that in both your press and online advertising. But for your public relations activity (see page 181) you might put out a story about how you overcame some obstacle (flood, thick snow, fuel shortage, whatever) to deliver on time to a needy customer. Such a story would be far more powerful than simply sending out a press release announcing that you deliver within 24 hours, which journalists are unlikely to take much interest in.

Something worth incorporating into your marketing campaign is a means of measuring the value of each activity. This could be as simple as asking every customer who calls how they heard about your company: Yellow Pages? Google ad? mail shot? exhibition? article in the local paper? This will allow you to judge the most cost-effective marketing activities, including the best places to advertise or get editorial coverage. Remember, however, what has just been said about the self-supporting nature of activities within a marketing campaign. Just because only a few customers say they contacted you after reading an article about your product, that doesn't mean your PR activity didn't make the rest of them more likely to respond to your advertisements.

**This is one of those things you just can't market –
there's nowhere to advertise it, no journalist will
write about it and I've not found a suitable mailing
list. All I can do is put it on the shelves and hope
people buy it.**

This Stupid Factor is something I actually heard a start-up CEO say!
Being in business is all about taking control and working to maximise
your chances of success – at no point do you want to throw your
hands in the air and rely on blind luck, especially with something as
crucial as getting people to buy what you're selling. But if you do find
you are out of ideas when it comes to marketing your product or
service, don't despair. Firstly, talk to the people in your own firm,
along with your suppliers and existing customers – these people will
be in as good a position as anyone to see potential marketing
opportunities. Then there's a wealth of free marketing advice to be
had from such sources as Business Link or any trade organisations
you've joined, not to mention the fellow business people you'll have
come across while you've been busy networking. And you can always
get the professionals in – hire an experienced marketing manager,
retain a marketing agency or employ a marketing consultant with
expertise relevant to your particular market. But before you take on
an agency or a consultant, shop around to find one that can at least
come up with a few concrete suggestions off the top of their head.
Definitely don't take on people who can only talk in abstract terms
using lots of marketing-speak (see **This consultant is using lots of
fancy lingo, so he must know what he's talking about**, page 217,
for some tips on how to avoid the sharks).

If you've spoken to all your colleagues and advisors and are still
desperate for ideas, but don't have the spare cash to pay for
professional assistance, you could always talk to marketing agencies
on a speculative basis, quizzing them for suggestions. This may be
seen as unethical, as you are effectively cadging some professional
advice without paying for it. But then again, the agencies should
welcome the opportunity to talk to a start-up and, if they are any good,
turn a window shopper into a new client.

After doing all this, if it still looks as if your target market is so
incredibly diffuse that no approach – ads, PR, direct mail, telesales,

Internet, sandwich boards – is likely to reach many of them, then you have to consider if your business stands much chance of succeeding. A notorious example of a customer group that is hard to reach successfully is small and home-based businesses, as it is difficult to identify any common factor, such as a particular publication their owners all read, that can be exploited by marketers. That's why, in desperation, many start-ups resort to the highly inelegant but low cost technique of bombarding any business in the phone book with faxes, emails and phone calls. Can you think of a better approach?

 I don't mind if this advertisement doesn't get much response from customers – it's really all about raising awareness and building brand image.

The number one priority for any start-up's advertising has to be to get a direct response from customers that will lead to a sale. Advertising is expensive, and new businesses simply cannot afford to do it unless it results in more sales. If your priority really is to increase awareness of your company and build brand image, there are far more cost-effective ways to do that, such as public relations.

Advertising

This is likely to be one of your more expensive options when it comes to marketing activities, once you take into account getting an advertisement or series of advertisements produced, perhaps employing an agency to determine the best places to put them and then paying for the actual medium (e.g. a page of a magazine or 30 seconds of television time). What's more, advertising is notoriously ineffective at influencing customer behaviour – when was the last time you ran out and bought something because of an ad? All of which means you need to think carefully about your use of advertising, to get maximum value from the high investment it requires.

Indeed, the decision by a start-up to advertise heavily can have a major impact on all aspects of the business, particularly the

---

amount of financing required in the first place. For example, if you choose to use television advertising to market your new product, you'll have to spend a considerable amount of money up front. It also means building a big margin into your price to cover this high cost and having all the infrastructure, such as a call centre, already in place to make best use of the big response you hope to get from your expensive campaign. So you will need much more start-up capital than if, for example, you choose to have a slow build up using a low-cost PR campaign (which might generate as much profit as a costly advertising-led campaign, even though it results in fewer units being sold).

Your decision to use advertising has to be based on whether it makes financial sense, and therefore needs to be incorporated directly into your business plan and its financial projections. In simplest terms, if an ad campaign will cost more than the profit you are likely to make from the sales it brings, then don't do it. Likewise, if a marketing campaign that doesn't use advertising won't generate enough sales to make a net profit – perhaps because you have high overheads – then that will be equally useless.

When it comes to producing your adverts, be they for print, radio, TV or the Internet, there are a few basic principles to keep in mind, whether you are putting the ad together yourself or briefing a freelance designer or advertising agency to do it. Firstly, what are the main points you want to put across with the advert? These should almost always include the benefits of your product or service to the customer – the exciting things that will actually motivate them to respond. In fact, with everything you say in your ad, you should imagine your customer reading or hearing it and think if they will say, *'Wow! That's great!'* or *'So what?'* These benefits should relate back to the core marketing messages mentioned earlier.

Secondly, make sure your ad will grab people's attention by having a headline that they cannot ignore. That means not having your company name followed by an empty or abstract statement. For example, 'Johnson's Limited – your first choice for beds' is meaningless, while 'Same day delivery on a wide choice of brand-name beds' immediately says what is important for the customer.

Thirdly, avoid being over-wordy with your advertisements: the general rule is that less is more. This is because you'll be lucky to even get people to notice your ad, and the odds of them then reading through a dozen paragraphs of text are very small. You need to think what the really important benefits are of what you are selling – the things you definitely want customers to remember after seeing or hearing the ad – and only mention these, rather than describing every detail of your product or service. Also, think carefully about who your customers are, and then make sure that the ad will appeal to them by using appropriate wording and images: never be stylish or clever for the sake of it.

Fourthly, if what you are marketing isn't immediately available in every shop in the country you should include what is called a 'call to action', whereby you tell customers what they should do next to either buy what you're selling or learn more about it. At the very least, be sure to include your web address and a phone number.

Deciding where to place your advertisement is at least as important as what it looks (or sounds) like. You need to maximise its effect by placing it in front of as many of the right people as possible. That means if a publication can't give you an independently verified figure for its circulation (an ABC, to use the technical term) then don't use them. Advertising sales people will ALWAYS exaggerate circulation if they can do so, with one common trick being to quote the number of magazines printed, which need not correspond at all with the number actually sold. And if they can't give you a breakdown on the sort of people reading their publication, tread very carefully, and use this lack of information to haggle down the cost of placing an ad. Indeed, you should always try hard to get a discount when placing an advertisement, even if the salespeople insist that they have to stick to the official rate card. One particularly effective way to reduce advertising costs is to wait until publications are about to go to print before buying space – they usually discount heavily to fill any remaining holes. It's tactics like this that may make the difference between profit and loss for your start-up.

I've already got loads of customers so I don't need to do any marketing.

When you're working flat out with the customers you already have, it's tempting to think that spending time and money on any marketing activity isn't worthwhile. But whether you're a sole trader or a high-growth with major funding, such an attitude could soon prove short-sighted and damaging to the future of your business.

What would happen if you were to lose customers – especially the big ones that make most of your profit? Or you decided to expand your business by taking on more customers? In both cases you could be in trouble if your entire marketing campaign has been on hold for some time. For a start, nobody will know who you are or what you do because you haven't kept up any kind of profile in your target market. And how will you even find new customers, given that you haven't been developing a database of prospects? (Incidentally, this illustrates the danger of being over-reliant on just a few big customers. In the short term they can make life easier for you because they remove the need to hunt down new customers, but in the long term they put your firm in a risky position – as very many entrepreneurs have found to their cost. So always have in mind, *'How would I cope if I lost my biggest customers?'*)

Even if you are confident you can raise your profile and get enough leads when you need them, there is another reason not to put marketing on hold. Are your customers the best you could possibly have? This isn't a reference to how they look or their friendliness on the telephone. What it does refer to is how profitable they are for you. Some customers will, inevitably, take up a lot of your time, even though they only ever place small orders, so that the profit you make from them is relatively small. Then there are the slow payers who give you cashflow nightmares. Wouldn't it make sound business sense to replace these problem customers with big spenders who pay on time? That can only happen, of course, if you actually have new customers to replace them with, and you will only find them through on-going marketing activity. See the next Stupid Factor for further discussion of this point.

Direct mail

However much you might personally be annoyed by the amount of junk mail that pours through your letterbox, the fact remains that direct mail can be a very efficient and cost-effective marketing option for start-ups. This is particularly so for businesses that sell to other business (business-to-business or B2B), especially those providing specialist products and services for which there is a small, well-defined market. In such cases, for a similar cost to an advertisement in a trade publication they typically could design, print and post a direct mail item to a big proportion of their potential customers. The generally accepted rule of thumb is that you should expect a two per cent response rate from direct mail (response means reacting in some meaningful way to the direct mail item, but not necessarily making a purchase). In fact, for big consumer campaigns, such as those conducted by financial services companies, two per cent would be considered staggeringly successful. However, with a carefully constructed campaign, particularly one that is business-to-business, you could do considerably better than that.

One of the big decisions you'll need to make is what to send. Brochures and catalogues are the most obvious choices, but you might also want to consider sending a newsletter. When these are well written and professionally produced they definitely get results.

Not only can they be used to highlight specific products and services that you sell, they also help build a positive overall impression of your business with the customer – something a standard catalogue would have difficulty doing. Newsletters are also a way of educating your customers about what it is you do, but without the pressure of the 'heavy sell' found in a typical company brochure.

Below are listed golden rules for success with direct mail. As you read them, remember that in direct mail, as with most things in marketing, it's the extra little bit of effort you put in that will make the difference between a campaign that's very successful and one that's a waste of time.

✓ Only use relevant, up-to-date and accurate lists

Your mailing list is critical to the success of your direct mail campaign. So don't be tempted to use any old list you stumble across that's going cheap, on the assumption that it only needs a few of the names and addresses to be accurate and relevant to be worth using. Instead, you should only use lists from reputable sources that were compiled within the past year. If you are in any doubt about the quality of a list you have already bought, don't be afraid to check and update it yourself by telephoning the people on it. This may sound like a chore, but it can greatly increase the effectiveness of your direct mail activity.

Make sure a list is relevant by applying all the criteria you use to define your target market, such as geographical location and demographic factors (e.g. income, gender, age and socioeconomic status, or business type and size). Also, a list should always include people's names – never send direct mail simply to an address. In addition, for business-to-business you must have a job title, and this has to relate to whatever it is you are selling. Sending a brochure on your contract cleaning services to the marketing director will get you nowhere.

In addition, consider compiling your own mailing lists. This can be done by keeping a careful record of people you come into contact with, ranging from anyone who telephones you for product details to people you meet at exhibitions. You can also pick up names and job titles from company websites, newspaper articles and the like. If you get into the habit of picking up names in this way you can soon develop a surprisingly effective list.

✓ Always include a personalised letter

You should do this whatever the main mail item is. Apart from anything else, getting a brochure or a price list in the post with no explanation can be downright confusing (*'Why have I been sent this? Do I owe them money or something?'*).

The letter itself should be written to grab and then hold the reader's attention, because you can't assume they will simply read everything that's sent to them. This is done by putting a subject line at the top they cannot ignore, such as one that implies the recipient will save lots of money by reading the whole letter. It's also important to include an interesting PS – folks just love a good post script and often read this first. You can liven up the main text using sub-headings, some bold type and also bullet points. If it is well written, a letter doesn't have to be short, but don't expect people to read much more than a side of A4. Make sure you relate the letter to whatever you have included in the mailing, perhaps by highlighting a particular product in the catalogue or an article in the newsletter you sent.

The key to successful selling is to engage the customer, and the best way to do that is to personalise the way you interact with them. Nobody likes to feel they're being sold to by a machine, and doing something as simple as putting their name in the greeting – Dear Mr J Jones rather than Dear Database Entry – and in the text can make your direct mail more compelling for your customers.

✓ **Make sure the mailing item looks professional and is relevant to the people you are sending it to**

Having gone to the trouble of getting a mailing list that bulls eyes your target market it would be a real pity to send something that isn't equally well tailored. Your standard brochure or catalogue, for example, may include many items that are not relevant to the people you have chosen to mail to. It would be unreasonable to expect them to wade through this literature to find the one or two things they might want to buy, so you should consider producing something specifically for your direct mail campaign. This will probably increase your costs, but could easily make the difference between getting a big response and no response at all.

If you are designing something to be used for direct mail, such as a newsletter, remember that your number one objective is not to have it decorating their waste basket five seconds after it lands on their doormat or desk. It therefore needs to have impact, perhaps by using a striking image and a headline that tells them why it is important for them to read this mail item.

Get any mail items, including the accompanying letter, double checked for mistakes such as misspellings, bad grammar, wrong phone numbers, invalid web addresses, incorrect prices, etc. There's nothing worse than going to the trouble of posting out to thousands of people something that says, '*Look at me, I'm slipshod and incompetent.*'

✓ **Include a call to action**

This is especially important with direct mail. There's virtually no chance that a direct mail item will be looked at a second time, so you need to get the recipient to respond immediately – usually by phoning a sales line, visiting a website or returning a form in the freepost envelope you've provided. A this-month-only discount, an implication of limited availability (*'Order now to avoid disappointment!'*), a special gift sent with the first hundred orders or a competition with an imminent deadline for entries may all seem cheesy, but if they make customers act within minutes of opening your envelope they will have been worth it.

Whatever you do, don't put obstacles in the way of customers finding out more about what you are selling or, worse still, make it anything other than effortless to place an order. Therefore, have your information/sales line number (consider getting a low rate or freephone number) and web address clearly visible on every page of the item you've sent.

✓ Create a timetable for your campaign and stick to it

Direct mail is great to coordinate with other marketing activities because you have so much control over it. The timing of advertising and editorial coverage are dictated by the vagaries of publishers' schedules, whereas direct mail goes out exactly when you want it to. You may need, for example, to have the mail arrive with business customers at the same time that an advertisement will appear in a trade publication or prior to a telemarketing campaign, so that you are getting maximum value from the marketing mix.

It is crucial that you do not slip on your timing – it's no use telling businesses about a special offer the day after it ends. This may seem an obvious point, but I've seen new businesses slip up on timing many times, so that their direct marketing campaign proved a complete waste.

I need every customer I can get.

If your start-up can only support a limited number of customers – perhaps because you are a freelancer with only your time to sell – then this definitely is not the case. The only customers you want are the ones that will give you maximum profit for minimum effort. This means you have to cherry pick the best customers, and turn away those who aren't likely to be worth your time. Of course, when your business has just started and you aren't at full capacity yet, turning away any kind of customer can be hard to do. But if you are confident that you will secure the 'good' customers reasonably soon, then saying 'no' now will leave you able to say 'yes' when you really want to.

Taking the idea of actively choosing your customers a step further, if ever you find yourself with 'bad' customers don't be afraid to replace them (as previously mentioned in **I'm already so busy I don't need to do any marketing**). Sacking customers may seem counter intuitive (and will probably be an uncomfortable experience the first time you do it), but if you can identify a business case for doing so then don't hesitate. Successful advertising agencies do this all the time.

How to sell

Undoubtedly, some people were born to sell – within seconds of meeting them they are your best mate and you'd buy anything off them. But if that's not you, don't despair, as most people can develop some sales ability, especially if they are passionate about what they're selling. In fact, if you have never even tried selling anything before you might be surprised at how naturally you take to it. Then again, if selling is something you know you cannot do at all, you must take this into account when you are planning your business. Most start-ups need someone who can sell, and if that isn't going to be you consider hiring a salesperson early on or partnering with someone who you know can sell. You might also consider partnering with a whole other organisation in a joint venture, whereby you use their salespeople to sell your product or service. Of course, the people doing this will expect a decent percentage of the revenue they generate for you, but it could still prove a very cost-effective way of overcoming your sales 'gap'.

Selling can take many forms – telesales, face-to-face, business-to-consumer, business-to-business – but there are some common principles that apply to all. The first step is usually to generate interest and desire in what you're selling. This is done by describing the features of the product and service and then explaining the benefits so that there is a pattern of feature-benefit, feature-benefit in your sales patter. Central to all of this is getting the customer to do most of the talking. That means asking lots of open questions that will tell you more about your customers, especially what their needs are and, therefore, which feature-benefit combinations are most relevant to them. If you do all the talking, it's more likely your customer will be turned off rather than excited about what you're selling.

 Also, make sure you close the sale, meaning that you actually ask if they want to make a purchase – something that new salespeople often forget to do. The best time to ask is when the customer has been exhibiting what are referred to as buying signs, such as asking questions about a product's features or wanting to know the cost of a service or even coming up with reasons for not buying. If you get a 'no' don't let this necessarily be the end of the sales pitch. It is often possible to turn a no into a yes if you still have the attention of the customer. So don't fear the no!

With selling over the phone there are a few extra rules you should follow. Always introduce yourself by stating your name and where you are calling from. When calling a business, establish that you are talking to the right person, namely the person who makes the purchasing decisions for what you are selling. Talking to someone who doesn't have this authority is usually a waste of time unless you have good reason to think he or she can influence the decision maker. Also, check the person at the other end has time to talk. If he or she is in the middle of a meeting with the chairman you aren't going to get very far, so enquire when would be a good time to ring back. And take the fag out of your mouth and talk clearly and at a reasonable pace – slow talking mumblers and frantic shouters never sell.

More generally, keep records of the people you have tried to sell to, including what was said, what was bought or, if they didn't buy anything this time, when they might be interested in making a purchase. All this is important if you intend to make sales calls to individuals or businesses on a regular basis. Having notes will mean you don't ring people too often and will give you a

→ → →

useful starting point when you do talk to them again, either on the phone or in person.

If you intend selling to big corporations there are some important points to keep in mind. The amount of time it takes to make even a low-value sale can be months, so take this into account in your business plan. Be prepared to talk to more than one person to get a sale – keep an eye out for gate keepers, influencers, recommenders and the like. In fact, being reliant on the support of just one or two people in a large company to make sales can put you in a very vulnerable position. You should try to build support across the board for your product or service, which is all part of the job of account management – the active maintenance of a profitable relationship with your customers. Good account management can soon become more important to your start-up than the ability to make one-off sales.

Note: there's lots of legislation associated with selling these days, which you need to take account of as you set up your sales and marketing operation. Stay up to date on these laws to avoid nasty fines and bad publicity. See Appendix 3 for a checklist of legal points to consider when communicating with and selling to potential customers.

⚠️ The newspapers will definitely be very interested in what I'm doing.

Will they really? As a former PR professional and a journalist, I've come across plenty of start-ups (particularly super-funded hi-techs and dotcoms) that believed national newspapers would be desperate to write about them. Unfortunately, this belief wasn't based on any understanding of what attracts journalists' attention and makes news.

Working out if your businesses should devote a lot of resources to public relations can be surprisingly difficult if you have no experience in this area. Small, lifestyle businesses that aren't doing anything original may still get national media coverage without spending a penny. Meanwhile, well-funded high-growth start-ups can struggle to get a mention, despite spending thousands with a PR agency. In addition, you may think that newspaper coverage is what your company needs, but in fact an article in a trade publication or a mention on local radio may be far more useful.

The important thing is not to commit a lot of money to a PR campaign, perhaps by hiring an agency or employing a full-time PR officer, without (a) knowing what your objectives are for it, and (b) having a good reason for thinking it can achieve them (that isn't based on your feelings of self-importance, i.e. *'If I was a newspaper journalist I'd want to write nice things about me and my company!'*).

Public Relations

This can be broadly defined as managing the perception of your business by the people that matter – customers, investors and others. What it means in practical terms for most start-ups is raising awareness and stimulating interest amongst these groups by obtaining coverage for the business in the media. To many people that sounds very similar to advertising, but in fact the two are very different. Firstly, mention of your products or services in an article carries much more weight with readers than an advertisement. Put simply, if a journalist says something is very good and worth buying, people are far more likely to believe that than an advert saying the same thing. Secondly, PR is much cheaper than advertising because you don't pay to have your business mentioned in an article or on a television programme. That's not to say there are no costs involved with PR, but these are considerably less than those of even the most modest ad campaign.

So, if PR is cheaper and more powerful than advertising should you concentrate on the former and not bother so much with the latter? Probably, but it's worth taking impartial advice on this, perhaps from someone in a similar business who conducted a PR campaign.

You should also try talking to some friendly, experienced journalists – you'll hopefully come across a few of these while you are doing all your networking. Talking to a PR agency is

---

another option, but they will almost always say the same thing – yes, you need PR, and we can do it for you!

Planning a PR campaign

As with everything else in business, a little bit of planning can make your PR activity much more productive. The first step is to think what exactly you want to get out of it – what are your PR objectives? These could include raising awareness amongst customers, letting business angels know that you are looking for investors or even publicising a specific event, such as an open day.

You also need to consider where you want all this fantastic (and free) media coverage. As a starting point, think about the media that your target audience is most likely to read/watch/listen to/surf, and avoid being overly-focused on the media that you happen to take an interest in. There should also be a timetable for your campaign which takes into account other marketing activities, season, your own availability to talk to the media (you don't want to send out a press release the day before you go on holiday) and factors within the business, such as the launch of a new product or a relocation.

Executing a PR campaign

So, how do you get positive coverage in your target media without going to the expense of employing a PR agency? Taking a DIY approach to PR is worth considering if you don't have the money to employ an agency or you want to test the water before spending big bucks on PR. Be warned: conducting a full-blown campaign involving newspapers, magazines, TV and radio can be very time consuming. However, a mention in the local papers is achievable with half-a-day's effort.

The first step is to get into the habit of thinking like a journalist. These folks are desperate for anyone to provide them with news and ideas for interesting articles. What they don't want (but what they have to spend all day dealing with) is businesses wasting their time doing neither. These firms, often despite employing a PR agency, tell journalists the sort of things that might appear in a brochure – we are great, we sell product X – but never in a publication. Instead, what you have to do is look for the real news hidden away amongst all the things that are happening within your business. For example, if you are looking to take on more employees then the news might be 'Employment boost for deprived area following success of hi-tech start-up'. What is not news is 'Microsift Ltd, the world leader in innovative software development for the telecommunications industry, is looking to fill vacancies in a number of departments after securing several new customers'.

Teach yourself to do this by reading through your target publications and identifying the kinds of stories that crop up which provide good publicity for a particular organisation. Usually these stories didn't make it into the news by chance – they will have been presented to journalists by the businesses mentioned.

Also, you should look at everything that's going on in your company for news ideas, not just the big things like product launches. As an example, employees raising money for charity probably has nothing to do with what your firm sells, but can be used to get positive coverage that would meet a PR objective such as raising awareness in the local community.

So how do you get this great news in front of the journalists? Answer: send them a press release. Think of this as a piece of direct mail which needs to grab the attention of the journos and prompt them to act by contacting you for more information. It should have a date at the top and the words PRESS RELEASE, plus an exciting headline in bold, then a single sentence in italics providing a concise summary of the press release. You should then have an opening paragraph which immediately tells the journalists what the news is. This is followed by further relevant information, a quote from someone such as a director or a customer, and then a brief final paragraph providing

→ → →

background information on your start-up. If you want to include a quote from someone outside your company the easiest way to go about this is to write the sort of thing you would like him (or her) to say, and then seek their approval for this to be attributed to him in your release. I have never known people to object to being provided with a suggested quote, as it saves them the trouble of having to think one up. Lastly, supply your contact details (telephone number, mobile number, email and website) so the journalists can quickly get hold of you for further information. The press release should then be posted or emailed, as preferred by the individual journalists. You can usually get journalists' contact details from the publications they work on.

You will greatly increase the chances of your press release being used if it closely relates to the media you are sending it to. This may mean adapting your headline and opening paragraph accordingly, for example to emphasise the local angle if sending it to the town newspaper and the industry angle if it goes to a trade publication. Another way to boost your success rate is by providing an interesting, good quality photograph to go with the release. You might want to use a press photographer to take the photo as he or she should have a perfect understanding of what newspapers and magazines want. If you don't know any suitable photographers then telephone your local newspaper and ask which freelance snappers they use. You can then either post a good quality print (put a caption and your contact details on the back) with your press release, state that a high resolution scan can be emailed if required or make the scan available for downloading from the Press section of your website. Remember that publications can't use the images you may already be using to decorate your website, as these will not be high-enough resolution to be printed in a magazine or newspaper.

Having distributed your press release you should follow it up with a phone call to the journalists, to make sure they spotted it amongst the dozens they receive each day. This can also be a chance to 'sell' the release to them by quickly summarising what it is about. Very few press releases get noticed without a follow-up call.

A very useful exercise is to take a close look at the actual media you want to get your business mentioned in. This should help you spot specific opportunities for coverage, such as through the letters page, a guest column you could offer to write for one issue or regular features, such as 'a day in the life'.

Finally, you might want to issue your press releases to more than just journalists. Sending them to important parties such as your major customers, bank manager, solicitor, accountant and investors can help ensure these people don't forget about you and build up a positive impression of your business.

PR agencies

If you truly believe PR will be an important part of your marketing strategy – perhaps by bringing in most of your sales leads – and you can justify the cost, then it may make sense to employ an agency. But beware: the standard of service provided by PR agencies varies tremendously. Some are so inefficient and inept that you would be better off doing the PR yourself. The really good ones, though, should be able to achieve coverage you didn't even imagine was possible for a lowly little start-up. It is, therefore, important to fully assess an agency before you take it on.

Not least, the PR agency must produce well-written press releases that get used by journalists. It should also efficiently distribute these releases to a wider range of media than you could do yourself. But to be of real value, it has to take the initiative in finding new ways to generate coverage. An agency that always waits for you to come up with ideas, and never seeks out opportunities for getting you written about, isn't worth bothering with.

You should gather evidence that an agency is able to do all of these things, and not take their word for it – talking to current and past clients is a good place to start. You also need to be sure that the agency's personnel are familiar with the individual journalists who will be key to the success of your PR campaign – which means that they speak to them and place news stories for their clients through them on a regular basis. Talking to these journalists yourself is the best way of determining this – if they haven't heard of the agency in question, then that's a real danger sign.

PR agencies can be used either on a continuous basis or for one-off projects, like a product launch. With the former you will pay a monthly retainer while with the latter there should be a single fee. In both cases you need to know what exactly you are getting for your money, such as a number of agency man-hours per week or press releases issued per month, and also what is not included, such as travel expenses and the cost of entertaining journalists.

 Good customer service is just answering the phone to customers within three rings and saying 'Have a nice day' at the end of the conversation.

Customer service can soon become more important to your start-up than sales, as it helps you retain customers (selling to existing customers is much cheaper than finding fresh ones) and maximise your revenue from them (such as by enabling you to 'cross-sell' secondary products and services). It can also help you gain new customers, as word spreads about what a great company you are to do business with. You should, therefore, have a strategy for customer service which goes beyond simply being polite on the telephone.

As an example of how taking customer service seriously can help a start-up to grow, TF Tuned Shox (**www.tftunedshox.com**) is a company which tunes, services and sells suspensions for top-of-the-line mountain bikes. It isn't the only company doing this, but unlike its rivals, it has managed to grow considerably over the past four years, with the workforce expanding from just its husband-and-wife founders to seven employees. Along the way it has cultivated an excellent reputation, with bikes being shipped to its Somerset workshop from as far as Canada and Australia.

Critical to TF's success has been not only a dedication to quality but also to customer service, with most bikes ready to be returned within 24 hours of receipt, much to their owners' appreciation. To do this, the company has had to invest in an extensive stock of spares – something which TF's competitors do not do, forcing them to wait for parts to arrive from manufacturers before they can work on a bike.

Providing a first-class service which both wins and retains customers can entail far more than politeness. For TF it went to the core of how the business was organised, with money being spent in an area (inventory) that may not be immediately associated with customer service.

The Internet

There are very few businesses that can't benefit from using the Internet as part of their marketing mix. Even a simple 'brochure' website can be useful, telling customers who you are, what you sell and providing contact details. But your website must look at least as professional as your printed marketing materials. Research has shown that people form an opinion about a site within a fraction of a second of opening it. That means if it looks cheap and uninviting, they will move on without a second thought. The mass use of broadband by businesses and consumers means there's no longer much excuse for having a dull site with no images.

One with a big, pretty picture but very little text will have a minimal ranking with search engines – even if you did pay someone with a ponytail a few thousand quid to design it. You may consider getting a search engine optimisation (SEO) professional to boost your site's chances of being at the top of any relevant searches, and also to help you determine what exactly those relevant searches are – you shouldn't be guessing which key words people are using.

However, you can find out most of what you need to know about SEO on the search engine websites themselves – including the importance of having other sites, such as web directories, linking back to yours. Most obviously, make sure your web address is on everything you have that is likely to be seen by customers, including your business cards, adverts, shop front, letterhead paper, brochures and any freebies you hand out such as mugs, pens and mouse mats.

Once your site is live it's vital that you keep it updated with the latest news and information about your firm and its products. If you don't do this, then someone returning to your site after a few months might get the impression that your company isn't going anywhere. As a start-up, this is far from the message you want to broadcast to the world, and people are unlikely to regularly revisit a site that never changes. At the very least you should put a blog (basically on online diary) on your site. Regularly adding and amending web pages also improves your site's search engine ranking.

Having got customers to your website you need to make the most of them being there. Your number one objective will be to get them to buy something through your site or phone you for more information. But at the very least you should try to get their email addresses. People might provide these to get something useful in return, such as an email newsletter, an ebook or notification of special offers. You must be sure to also get them to agree to you using their email addresses for more general marketing purposes. The tick box you provide for this purpose can, sneakily, be pre-ticked to say they agree, but it must be possible for them to untick it. (They should also be able to easily cancel this agreement at a later date. In addition, any emails you send must include your contact details and a valid return email address.) The point is that email can be an important marketing tool for your business. If, for example, you can tell most of your customers about a new product or service simply with an email, then you will be saving yourself an enormous amount of time and money. So you should quickly get into the habit of collecting and storing email addresses at any and all opportunities. Incidentally, the law about getting people's agreement to be emailed for commercial purposes only applies to private email addresses – there is no such restriction for business email addresses.

Finally, pay-per-click advertising has emerged as one of the most powerful marketing tools the Internet has to offer. It involves paying to have an advertisement appear at the top of search engine listings, though in the case of Google you only pay if someone clicks on your ad. This system lets you target your marketing effort directly at potential customers, and is, therefore, much more efficient than conventional advertising. One tip is to not always pick the most obvious search terms to trigger the listing of your advert. As well as costing the most to use (pay-per-click involves bidding to use search terms), very general search terms may not deliver serious buyers interested in your particular offering. The trick is to constantly experiment with search terms (along with every other aspect of your pay-per-click campaign) to see what brings the most sales.

12

Start-up Stories: Publish and Be Damned

Magazine publishing is a notoriously difficult game to get right and make money from. Yet each year, like lambs to the slaughter, people set up yet more glossies that will fold within months. They are often driven on by financial projections which show that even with only a modest level of sales, there's a fortune to be had from being on the newsagent's shelf. And what could be cooler than having your very own magazine to show friends at dinner parties?

But as with everything in business, if it was that easy everyone would be doing it. For students of the Stupid Factor this is very fertile ground, and whatever sort of business you want to start, there is much of value to be learned here. What follows are the sad tales of two magazines I was employed by (though I like to think that wasn't a factor in their downfall). The first illustrates how even with a thoughtful, calculated approach, it is still possible to fall at the final hurdle. The second shows how Stupid Factors can build up over time so that even the best business idea is doomed to fail, no matter how much money eventually gets spent on it.

IT Marketing

The big success stories in magazine publishing always involve finding and exploiting a gap in the market. *Hello!* and *Loaded* may not seem to have much in common, but each was the first of its kind, tapping into a whole new magazine market – celebrity-obsessed genteel women and beer-obsessed yobbish men respectively. And it was with this kind of thinking in mind that Toby Chapman-Dawe set about coming up with his own idea for a magazine.

Toby ran a successful writing and design agency producing brochures and other literature for information technology (IT) companies such as IBM. He had previously worked for publishing house Centaur which had boasted numerous successes, including the trade title *Money Marketing*. This is a controlled circulation weekly newspaper for the financial services market, principally insurance, life and pensions brokers. While this may not sound as exciting as a lad's mag, it made Centaur lots of money, but not in the way that was expected. It was assumed most of the profit would come from display advertising – big ads in amongst the editorial (the magazine was distributed free of charge, so there was no money to be made from sales). But instead it came from the classified recruitment adverts at the back of the paper, with over half-a-dozen salespeople eventually employed to fill these pages (including the future author of *Stupid Factor*). Toby saw that *Money Marketing's* success had come from its efficient exploitation of an industry niche with strong recruitment pressures (there's always a demand for salespeople in financial services) that had so far been ignored – could he do something similar?

The IT and telecommunications market in the UK is enormous, and is served by an equally vast army of marketing professionals – PR officers, marketing managers, product managers, salespeople, plus innumerable PR, advertising and marketing agencies, many of which specialise in the technology sector. How about a controlled circulation weekly magazine for all these sparky men and women? There were already general marketing titles, *Marketing* and *Marketing Week*, but nothing specific to IT. Plus, people with the knowledge and skill to work in this sector were in short supply, so companies were constantly on the search for personnel.

Toby was excited by the prospect of being the first to cater exclusively to this apparently very lucrative market, but before launching a magazine he needed to know a lot more. He paid a research company to look at existing magazines and measure the value of the advertising – both display and recruitment – they carried that would be relevant to the new publication. This gave Toby an indication of the size of his potential advertising market. He saw that if he acquired just ten per cent of it he would be in profit, although he reckoned on getting nearer to 40 per cent if the new magazine dominated the marketplace.

The research completed, it was now possible for him both to prepare a detailed business plan that could be used to attract investors, and to develop a sales pitch to potential advertisers. He was also able to make an informed assessment of the most suitable model for the publication, eventually choosing controlled/free circulation. The sacrifice in sales revenue, he calculated, would be more than compensated for by the higher advertising revenue he would bring in by having a magazine with a guaranteed circulation amongst its target readership.

It's worth noting that Toby originally assumed the market research would take three months. However, when he analysed the figures the researchers provided he found himself wanting even more information. For example, he saw that revenues would be higher if end companies were buying advertising space to recruit directly, rather than if it were bought by recruitment agencies, which would cram a greater number of vacancies into a given space. This led him to ask for greater detail about which businesses were placing what recruitment advertisements. The end result was that it took a year to complete the research.

A benefit of his publishing background was that Chapman-Dawe already knew, or could arrange to be introduced to, potential investors. His pitch to them was that the new magazine would be built up, then either joined by a range of sister titles (so that he would be building a publishing house) or, if the price was right, it would be sold to a larger publisher that felt it could further exploit the title. There was also an intention to build a brand around *IT Marketing*, as the magazine would eventually be called. For example, there could be IT Marketing-branded events such as industry conferences and exhibitions. These activities, marketed through the magazine, had the potential to bring high revenues for the publishing company, so that

IT Marketing itself would only need to make a minimal profit. With a strong pitch like this, Toby soon found investors willing to fund the launch of the magazine (though they weren't willing to provide much non-financial support, such as practical help and advice on running the business).

In no time, or so it seemed, the investor agreements were signed, he'd set up a limited company and the business systems were in place, including an accounting package that gave Toby a detailed, up-to-the minute view of the firm's finances. He recruited an editor he'd lined up months before, and she in turn hired a sub-editor. Most of the writing was to be done by freelance journalists to begin with, to minimise fixed overheads. A dummy issue was created and then the magazine was to be launched properly just before summer, which would provide two clear months to sell advertising space before the slow season when everyone who mattered would be off on holiday. Almost the very last act before this was to hire a couple of sales executives. These two young men had little relevant experience but bags of enthusiasm, and given that time was now running short Chapman-Dawe took them on.

The first two issues met with an enthusiastic reception from readers, and although not much advertising had been sold, Toby wasn't too concerned: *'These were just an awareness campaign,'* he says, and not expected to make a profit. But when sales subsequently failed to take off, he began to get worried. Some minor changes were made to the magazine's editorial style but it was obvious that this wasn't where the real problem lay. Toby needed to galvanise the sales team into winning more business, but try as he might he couldn't get any improvement here. He also tried to secure further funding from new investors and, later, find some sort of exit route (such as a trade sale to another publisher) to help the original investors, but had no joy either way.

With the magazine losing £20,000 a week, it soon reached the point where Toby could see, through his close tracking of the business's finances, that it was just four weeks from running out of money. In a final bid, the original sales team was laid off and an experienced media salesman brought in, which resulted immediately in increased sales.

But the growth rate of sales was too slow, Toby judged, to ever have a hope of making enough profit to pay off the publication's mounting debts. It was, therefore, decided to halt the search for further investment and close the company down – despite the last issue being the first one to come close to making an operating profit (i.e. cover the immediate costs of production and distribution) with sales of £12,000. It was a very sad day for all concerned, as a great idea that a lot of people had worked very hard on, and which had come so very close to being a success, finally ended in failure after just six months, at a total cost of £250,000.

So how had things gone so wrong so quickly? Was it a lack of financial planning or poor cost control? Chapman-Dawe doesn't think so, with direct production costs of £10,000 per issue and a further £8,000 in overheads matching his initial budget; even an estimation of ten per cent bad debt (companies not paying for their advertising space) proved very accurate. And at the time, it certainly didn't appear that there was any extravagant spending on *IT Marketing*, which was put together in the founder's flat alongside his other business, which also provided the design and layout expertise to put the magazine together.

Was it basically a bad idea for a publication? Judging by the enthusiastic reaction of the readers, along with the strong interest shown by rival publishers (one of which even put out a similar magazine, *MarketingIT*, just in advance of *IT Marketing's* first issue, though this was never a direct competitor), it's hard to believe so. Plus, the initial research had clearly shown there was a strong market for the magazine. Instead, the problems, by Toby's own admission, lay in two other areas – recruitment and financing.

Regarding recruitment, this centred on the advertising sales department, with Toby commenting, *'I didn't leave enough time to hire and review the progress of the sales staff. I'd rather have put off launching until I had the right people, but in the rush to get going these things acquire their own logic.'* Looking back, he feels he *'wasn't ruthless enough'* with his recruitment. It would also have been useful to have an advertising sales director, possibly an investor, who could have taken charge of this crucial business function. Toby admits this wasn't a strong area for him, saying, *'The salesmen were always nearly succeeding, but I couldn't see what it was they were getting wrong and then provide the necessary training.'*

Why exactly did he hire such inexperienced people to such important roles? He did so because this was what he had done previously (and successfully) in his business career, considering enthusiasm to be more important than experience. But in all these cases it had been for roles such as writing, editing and design, which he was personally very experienced in and where he could provide guidance. And so he had learnt the wrong lesson regarding experience and proven expertise, and came a cropper when hiring for a job role – sales – he wasn't an expert in. Toby also feels he shouldn't have necessarily been running the whole show, even though *IT Marketing* was his idea: he should have hired a publisher, and factored that cost into his plans, instead of doing the job himself. After all, he would have been more than busy enough running his writing and design company.

As for financing, Toby says, *'A good idea would have been to spend more time earlier on finding investors who knew about publishing. Ideally, I'd have found someone who had set up a similar company and who knew about getting funding. Also, having more investors would have provided me more opinions on how to run the business. After all, I wasn't afraid to lose some of my equity to make the business a success. As it was, I worked too much in isolation. But the biggest lesson I learnt was: stick to what you are good at, hire the best people for everything else.'*

One thing's for sure, waiting for the advertising sales crises to deepen before looking hard for extra funding didn't help matters; Toby wasn't able to attract additional investors under these circumstances. The sweet spot for finding these people would surely have been straight after the first few issues were printed, when there was a tangible product to impress them with (i.e. copies of the magazine) and finances that didn't yet look too dire. The money raised could then have been spent on hiring more and better sales personnel. Hoping that sales would improve fast enough without this extra investment was an unnecessary gamble – and one that didn't pay off.

Motorcycle Voyager Ltd

Like Toby Chapman-Dawe, Laurence 'Lolly' Turner also thought he saw a lucrative gap in the publishing market, but in his case it was for a special interest consumer magazine rather than a trade publication. This short, fat and irrepressibly jolly salesman in his mid-forties is a keen biker who loves nothing better than to travel around Europe on his two-wheeled stallion. In fact, his passion for long-distance riding led to him looking at newsagents' shelves and noticing that while there were plenty of different motorcycle magazines for sale, there were none specifically catering to his interest. Yes, there were glossy mags that talked about the newest bikes or the fastest bikes or classic bikes or dirt bikes – but none that concentrated on motorcycle touring.

Laurence soon saw this was an excellent business opportunity, but before he could do anything with it he needed to find a partner. This person would have to both share the cost of publishing a new magazine, and also help him with an aspect of running a business that he knew he would find difficult – financial management. Laurence freely admits that numbers aren't his strong point – *'I find all that accounts stuff really boring,'* he once told me – and that creating cashflow projections, calculating breakeven points and working out budgets would be beyond him.

Very conveniently, Turner's ex-boss, Chris Cave, was a qualified accountant in his early fifties with lots of spare cash to invest, thanks to previous business successes. Without much difficulty, Laurence was able to convince Chris to go into business with him. Even with sales well below those of existing bike magazines, Chris saw that it could generate considerable revenue, and seemed an easy way to make a good return on a relatively small upfront investment. So why shouldn't he back Lolly's big idea?

Cave had previously made his money helping companies and their employees avoid paying tax through various schemes (Lolly had been one of his salespeople). He now worked in film financing, which while it may have sounded more glamorous, was still largely about helping people reduce their tax bills. It's also worth pointing out that Chris wasn't a biker and had never had anything to do with publishing beyond reading his morning paper. But this lack of industry experience or affinity with the subject of the magazine didn't matter too much to him. For a start, Laurence had a background in publishing, having sold advertising space on the trade publication *Banking Technology* ten years previously, so that would compensate for his inexperience. Also, he'd known nothing about film producing when he'd moved into that area, but he'd eventually made a success of it. In fact, if he'd known how hard producing films would be he probably wouldn't have tried it, so perhaps a certain amount of ignorance was actually an advantage. And finally, he would learn to ride a bike – after all, how difficult could that be? As it turned out, Laurence's knowledge of publishing would prove all too thin, while Chris's ignorance wouldn't be any kind of virtue. Worst of all, after two failed attempts, Chris had to give up trying to pass his bike test.

Despite the magnitude of the task in hand – producing, printing, distributing and marketing a brand new bi-monthly magazine – no business plan was written, although Chris did do detailed financial projections. A small amount of market research was conducted which indicated that *Motorcycle Voyager* certainly had plenty of potential to make money. It was discovered that there were three million motorcycle license holders in the UK, and that well over 150,000 crossings were made to Europe by bikers each year, so the market for the magazine was huge.

In addition, the two founders took an exhibition stand at Britain's biggest biking event. Not only did this give them a chance to advance promote the magazine, but they could also conduct more qualitative market research. That meant asking individual bikers if they would be interested in a touring magazine and if so, what they would want to see in it. The results of this informal research were very positive, with many bikers saying they would definitely consider buying such a publication.

It was decided early on that *Motorcycle Voyager* needed to be a newsstand publication, rather than subscription only. This meant before they could really get going with the magazine they had to be sure they could get it distributed and in the shops. Key to this was obtaining a commitment from the UK's number one magazine retailer, WH Smith, to take the publication. This they achieved, with the buyer at WH Smith commenting that he saw *Motorcycle Voyager* as being a 'lifestyle' publication rather than simply a special interest magazine, which made it far more attractive to the retailer – and more likely to succeed. This was an important development for the company, and effectively gave the green light to producing the magazine.

An important next step was to hire an editor. After advertising the post they were deluged with applicants, one of whom, Jon Orson, immediately seemed ideal. He was a very experienced motorcycle journalist who had edited one of the UK's biggest selling bike mags. More recently, he had also published his own motorcycle magazine, although this had failed after just a year. But when Laurence and Chris interviewed Jon, things didn't go well. The partners would later tell me that they found him rude, belligerent and generally unpleasant – he also didn't seem very keen on the magazine. Hiring him didn't appear an option, but a few days later they received a carefully composed email from him in which he explained both his enthusiasm for the project and how he was undoubtedly their best choice in the country for the post of editor. He also stated that he could easily work from his home office using the equipment he'd already bought for his own magazine. Amazingly, on the basis of this email, the pair took him on for this crucial position with a salary that was well above the market rate. This was despite the fact that they had not liked at all what they had seen and heard at the interview. Perhaps it just seemed the easiest option – hiring someone who was experienced and available immediately, rather than continuing the search.

Predictably (well, predictable to keen students of the Stupid Factor), things did not go well with Jon. Laurence and Chris later told me he was as rude and belligerent when he became an employee as he had been at the interview. Jon never visited the company's office in Bristol, preferring to work exclusively from home 120 miles away, so that all communication was by telephone or meetings at motorway service stations. More disturbingly, the partners began to feel he wasn't making much progress getting the magazine ready for print, with only a couple of articles being produced. After just two-and-a-half months, Laurence and Chris had had enough and sacked Jon.

A surly disposition and possibly being a bit slow at doing the job aren't very strong reasons for summary dismissal (especially if you have neglected to get your employee to sign an employment contract), so unsurprisingly Jon started proceedings to take the company to an Industrial Tribunal to obtain pay in lieu of notice. Chris and Laurence hired a solicitor to fight the case, but were shocked to discover that you can't fire someone just for not doing their job very well. So, as is typical in these situations, after negotiations through ACAS (Arbitrations and Conciliation Service) a compromise was reached, and Jon received a settlement of over £4,000 from Motorcycle Voyager Ltd. (Very few disputes get as far as being heard by the Tribunal itself.)

Laurence would later claim that he had been very dubious about hiring Jon following the interview, and that it was Chris who was won over by the email. This was to become something of a theme with Turner, as he repeatedly pushed the blame for bad decisions onto his partner, despite the fact he was the majority shareholder and self-styled CEO. This unwillingness to accept personal responsibility only hindered the company's development over the coming months.

In any event, after three months, the dynamic duo had managed to spend a lot of money – Jon's salary and expenses, solicitor's fees, and Jon's settlement – but had absolutely nothing to show for it. They were back at square one and needed, once again, to hire an editor...

My involvement in the saga of *Motorcycle Voyager* began when I saw a tiny advertisement for an 'editor/senior journalist' in the recruitment section of *The Guardian*. I emailed my CV and a few days later got a reply from a Laurence Turner saying he was interested in interviewing me for the job. A couple of weeks then passed without hearing anything, so that I had to send another email asking if we could actually set up the interview. A week later and I arrived by bike at the shabby, dusty offices of Motorcycle Voyager Ltd in Lawrence Hill, a district of Bristol so grim it has special status with the local RDA (although Chris and Laurence were never to exploit that fact to obtain grant funding). The interview went well, with Laurence liking my article ideas for the magazine, and for some reason he was also very impressed that I'd changed out of my bike leathers and into a suit. I was to have a second interview with him and Chris at a hotel near where I lived in London.

The day before the scheduled date of the interview Laurence rang to say that he and Chris were *'still okay to meet me at the hotel this afternoon'*. Laurence had got the wrong day for the interview, but I was still able to meet up with them that afternoon. Except Chris went to the wrong hotel, so he arrived an hour late for the interview. When, a few weeks later, they finally got around to offering me the job, I could only hope that this performance wasn't typical of how they operated.

Following the Jon experience, the pair were understandably keen that I relocate to Bristol to work out of their office, which I was more than happy to do. Trouble was, they made little preparation for having an employee in their midst, even though I didn't actually move till three months after joining the company. True, they had a flaky PC (thrown together by a hobbit-like creature employed on a very casual basis to provide IT support for Chris's various ventures), a crackly old telephone and a rickety desk ready for me, but, crucially, no broadband Internet access. In the world of publishing, this is usually considered vital, and I would have to struggle for months with a slow but very expensive dial-up connection before getting broadband. I also wasn't given either an employment contract (although I did receive my written terms of employment), an employee handbook or, remarkably, a written editorial brief for the magazine itself. Almost all I had to go on when planning the first issue was the publication's title (motorcycles... voyaging...) and random comments from Laurence, which usually related to his desire to have a pretty lady on the cover and lots of articles on his favourite activity, camping.

But it wasn't this lack of preparation that had me worried in the first few months. From the start, I'd been told more investors would be sought for the company, but after relocating to Bristol, I was told this wouldn't be happening. This meant that the two would each be providing half the total start-up capital of £50,000, with Chris having a 49 per cent share in Motorcycle Voyager Ltd and Laurence 51 per cent. I was concerned as soon as I heard about the no-other-investors decision, as it's well known that publishing is a risky business at the best of times, and that it generally takes a lot more time and money than first-time publishers expect to get a new title established (something I'd learned at *IT Marketing*, and which I tried to explain to Chris when I first met him). Between them, would these two jokers really have the funds, not to mention the expertise, to get *Motorcycle Voyager* motoring?

Another thing that soon had me nervous was Laurence's tendency not to follow through on things he said he'd do. As an example, he was responsible for arranging an insurance policy that would cover anyone in the company, plus the freelance journalists we would be using, riding a motorcycle as part of their work for the magazine. This was an important asset for the business to acquire, as without it we wouldn't be able to review new bikes. But weeks and months passed and a policy still wasn't in place, despite Turner claiming he'd spoken to an insurer who'd told him it would be trivial to set up. In reality, it proved very difficult to obtain such a policy, and my own bike ended up featuring heavily in the first issue of the magazine – as it was the only one I was insured to ride!

I couldn't help thinking that this and numerous similar incidents resulted from Laurence believing that a single phone call was all that was needed to solve any problem or get anything done. But in business that is rarely the case, and he just didn't seem prepared for the big effort (nor possess the endless determination) required to do everything needed to set up a successful business. It also soon became obvious that he had little organisational ability, which on several occasions led to the world's worst publishing sin being committed: booked advertisements failing to appear in the magazine (as well as being CEO and publisher, Laurence was also the advertising sales director). To keep track of who was advertising in *Motorcycle Voyager* all he had was a simple list of advertisers which he amended for each issue – a system ripe for error. On one particularly glorious occasion he got confused by two advertisers with vaguely similar names, one of which had stopped using the magazine. Inevitably, he put the wrong advert in the publication, leaving out the one from the advertiser that had actually made the booking. I can now testify from personal experience that a small business will always struggle if there is a key member of the team like Laurence – someone unwilling to accept their shortcomings as a manager and take positive steps to deal with them.

It is probably no surprise to find that as launch date neared I became increasingly concerned about the aspects of the magazine that were outside my direct control as the editor. So I arranged a crisis meeting with the directors to discuss these, in particular the lack of advertising booked for the first issue, and the instinctive feeling that not enough effort was being put into organising distribution. The only problem was that the duo couldn't see that there was a crisis. Laurence made vague comments about more advertising being booked soon, which seemed to satisfy Chris. Meanwhile, Chris felt that the distribution was in hand – after all, they'd had one meeting with WH Smith and appointed a distributor (the organisation that takes orders from wholesalers and physically gets the magazines out to them). Maintaining ongoing contact with our most important retailer and getting directly involved in the distribution process weren't necessary, apparently. I should also have asked what would be done to market the magazine, as that too would soon prove an important factor in the future of the publication.

At the same meeting, the subject of the Cannes Film Festival came up. Chris's movie production company would be attending it, so the suggestion was made of riding bikes to the event in the South of France and writing an article based on the trip. This sounded a great idea, except that the pair then started talking about hiring a luxury yacht and selling tickets to parties that they would hold on board during the Festival. When I commented that we should concentrate solely on getting the magazine published the pair seemed perplexed. They genuinely couldn't understand why I wasn't as excited as they were by this obvious money-spinning opportunity. Such easy distraction from the task in hand was to become a hallmark of Chris and Laurence's management style. Fortunately, in this case it didn't lead to any harm – the road trip to the Festival went ahead, but no floating parties were organised.

A couple of weeks later, and less than a month before the launch date for *Motorcycle Voyager*, there was finally a realisation that something needed to be done about getting advertising booked in the first issue. It was now obvious that, on his own, Laurence was never going to sell much space, and so a freelance ad salesman was hurriedly hired. Given their previous troubles with their home-working first editor, I thought it natural that they'd get someone local who they could closely supervise by having them work from the office. But once again, they went for the quick and easy option of someone available immediately – but with little track record in media sales and located a hundred miles from HQ.

In November 2002, five months after I'd taken over as editor, the magazine finally went on sale – but not to any great fanfare. True, it was officially launched at the International Motorcycle and Scooter Show at the NEC in Birmingham, which was a great way of ensuring thousands of bikers at least had the chance to see it and buy it (the company had a stand at the event). But otherwise, there was no marketing done for the magazine – no advertising, no PR campaign, no posters, no direct mail, no website, nothing. Most bikers would only know about it if they walked into a shop and happened to spot one of the 50,000 copes that had been printed, on the shelf (which, it'd soon be revealed, would be even harder than it sounded).

That isn't to say there had never been any thought about actively promoting the magazine. There was an arrangement with a motorcycle insurance company that its customers would be given the chance to subscribe at a discount when they took out a policy. This was a great opportunity to get *Motorcycle Voyager* off to a flying start, but for no obvious reason other than a lack of will, the directors had not yet followed through on this by producing a direct marketing piece to send out to policy holders. In fact, it would take a whole year before a basic leaflet was created, which would prove far too little too late with regard to marketing. Over the lifetime of the magazine the only significant promotional activity would be taking stands at motorcycle shows. While there was nothing wrong with this activity as such – and it did pick up subscribers – it could only ever reach a tiny proportion of the magazine's market.

The weeks that followed the launch were ones of never-to-berepeated optimism and excitement. At the NEC, there had been strong interest in the magazine and plenty of sales; I received numerous letters to the editor praising the publication; and we were gaining up to a dozen more subscribers each day. Best of all, the distributor was confident we had sold at least 25,000 copies (although they couldn't be certain, as the barcode Laurence had put on the cover didn't work), which would see the founders getting almost all their initial investment back. This would be despite selling little more than £4,000 of advertising, which was well below what might have been expected for a 98-page newsstand magazine.

Indeed, Chris got so excited he made plans to start a motorcycle holiday company, MV Tours, which would cash in on the apparent instant success of the publication. MV Tours would provide bikers with motorcycles for trips around the Balkans and would be led by Yuri, Chris's young Croatian friend who had been hired by the directors as a journalist before I became editor. (I eventually discovered his usual occupation was pizza delivery and that he had never worked as a journalist before. More significantly, he was also only barely literate in English – his articles could easily have been the work of a ten-year-old – so that I soon had to refuse to use him as a correspondent, much to Chris's and Yuri's disappointment.) The fact that neither Yuri nor Chris had any experience or knowledge of the holiday industry, beyond going on holiday themselves, seemed irrelevant, and certainly no barrier to Chris ordering a fleet of BMW bikes and placing an advertisement in the following issue of the magazine.

When the second issue of the magazine went on sale two months later (*Motorcycle Voyager* was initially bi-monthly) there was still no final count on sales of the first issue. What's more, there was a recurrence of the barcode problem with issue two. So it wasn't until I was in the closing stages of putting issue three together that the terrible truth came out: issue one had sold just 8,000 copies, which would bring in just £13,600 (£1.70 per copy). Added to the £6,000 or so made from advertising and subscriptions, this still left around £30,000 of start-up capital that hadn't been recovered.

It's worth noting that the cost of starting up the company and producing the first issue actually cost considerably more than £50,000. But with careful cashflow management – i.e. not paying all bills immediately and receiving revenues from the first issue as quickly as possible – Chris was confident that was all the money the company required to get started. To that end, he arranged extended payment terms with the printer, with a third of the print cost being paid each month for three months after printing. This was rather than the total cost being invoiced for immediate payment, well before money would come in from advertisers and shop sales. But by not coming even close to making a gross profit with the first issue (i.e. covering design, print and editorial costs) all Chris's financial plans were thrown into disarray, so that more money had to be found to continue producing the magazine. (See the financial projections for *Honeymoons* magazine, page 72, for further insight into cashflow management.)

Some relief came from the distributor already having given the company money for sales of the mag based on its flawed estimate of 25,000, and that it wouldn't demand the overpayment to be returned. But perhaps that seemed only fair after the distributor admitted that 20,000 magazines had never left the warehouse. These were copies that no wholesaler or retailer had asked for, but which it instructed Chris and Laurence to print as a contingency – spare copies to distribute if shops and wholesalers ran out. Except that the distributor supposedly didn't actually tell the duo that these were a contingency, even though the printing of them would cost nearly £20,000 – almost half the start-up capital.

The financial failure of the first issue – and the lack of any plan to deal with it, such as the recruitment of additional investors – would prove a blow from which Motorcycle Voyager Ltd never really recovered. To a large part it would now be dependent on further cash injections from Chris to survive, who by his own admission turned from being financial director to financier. The real problem was that this money was only ever given reluctantly by Chris, when it was absolutely needed to get the magazine printed. That meant there was never a useful sum of working capital that could be used to develop the business. In fact, by supplying cash in a piecemeal fashion Chris probably ended up losing more money than if he'd bitten the bullet and put in a hefty sum straight after learning the sales figure for issue one.

After some vacillation, it was decided to continue with the magazine in the hope that sales would somehow increase, although Chris did abandon the MV Tours project. They also decided to directly employ an advertising salesperson to replace the independent sales consultant, whom it was decided wasn't flogging enough space. To do this they went to a local recruitment agency and after several interviews asked Barry, an experienced salesman in his late thirties, to do a trial workday. Following this he was taken on as a full-time employee to work from the Lawrence Hill office.

It seemed that my employers were finally learning from their past mistakes, and were taking on someone with a view to properly managing him. But this hope was soon shattered when Barry arrived for his first proper day of work to find he had no desk and computer of his own – he had to share Laurence's. Worse still, the only help he was given to get started in his new job was to be handed assorted bits of paper – adverts torn from other bike magazines and pages pulled from directories – and told to ring any phone numbers he could find on these. There was no database of leads to work through, and not even the sales director, Laurence, present to show him the ropes and answer questions he might have about the magazine.

Needless to say, Barry was very unimpressed by this lack of organisation (or even basic consideration for a new employee) and after four days he resigned. However, Chris successfully convinced him not to leave – except that Barry refused to work in the office. He said Lawrence Hill was too dangerous, claiming he'd been mugged on the bus home. Barry, therefore, would now be working from home.

Over the next two months, Barry didn't sell any advertising space, except for a very small amount on the handful of days he took his life into his hands and risked a trip to the office. During this time Laurence struggled to manage the never-present Barry, finding him almost impossible to contact by telephone. On top of this, the directors had hired him without directly informing his recruitment agency. When the agency eventually discovered he'd become an employee, Motorcycle Voyager Ltd had no option but to pay an expensive recruitment fee for its unproductive salesman – or risk being taken to court for breach of contract.

After he received his second salary cheque Barry simply disappeared, never to be heard from again. Once more, the magazine was left with only one employee – me! – and in desperate need of a media salesperson. But that wasn't the only crisis to suddenly rock the company: when the third edition of *Motorcycle Voyager* arrived from the printer it looked terrible.

Before I became editor, the directors had already chosen a Coventry-based design house to produce the magazine – and there were problems from the start. Quite apart from the practical difficulties of using designers based a hundred miles from my office, it was obvious they had very little experience of laying out magazines. And when the first issue was printed it certainly didn't look as good as I'd hoped. The second issue was greatly improved, but the third issue was even worse than the first, filled with hopelessly blurred and grainy pictures (despite the photographs I'd supplied being crystal clear). Immediately, I took the initiative to find new designers, and after just two weeks I'd located an excellent design company within walking distance of the office that specialised in producing magazines. Better yet, it would charge £3,000 an issue – half the price of the Coventry bunch. At the same time, Laurence found a new printer that could print *Motorcycle Voyager* for 47p per copy – almost half what we'd previously paid. Now the full extent of the folly committed in the early days of the magazine was revealed – the company had been paying double for its most important services. Had we paid the lower prices from the start, and not printed the pointless 20,000 contingency copies, the first issue would actually have covered its costs; issue two, which sold 10,000 copies on a smaller print run of 34,000, would even have made an operating profit.

Once again, Laurence and Chris had to hire an ad salesperson – and this time got it right! They took on an experienced media salesman, Steve, who'd trained with a major publisher, as an office-based employee, and even gave him his own desk and computer. He quickly proved very capable, increasing ad sales to almost £20,000 per issue, even as circulation dropped dismally to around 5,500. So were the two bosses finally learning from their mistakes and giving the magazine a fighting chance?

From soon after issue one was distributed, Laurence and Chris became increasingly excited about the North America market. This stemmed from the distributor sending several thousand copies of the mag to the US and Canada, and then reporting that it was apparently selling well there. The directors soon began to think they might make more money from selling *Motorcycle Voyager* there than in the UK.

At about the time that Steve was hired, the pair was approached by consultants, who claimed they could help the company exploit the North America market by setting up joint ventures with media organisations based there. They also believed they could find investors for the business as well as providing general marketing consultancy. On the basis of a proposal packed full of marketing jargon – and against my advice – the consultants were soon hired at a rate of £3,500 per month. This was money they would get irrespective of actually finding investors or setting up joint ventures. After two months the consultants produced a marketing report recommending, so Laurence later told me, that the company exploit the *Motorcycle Voyager* brand by setting up a website – and pay them to create it. Seven thousand pounds might seem rather a lot for this kind of advice, especially as no investors were found or media deals set up. On top of that, there was in-house marketing expertise, in the form of myself and Steve, that could have been exploited for free. Indeed, Steve later came close to setting up a lucrative licensing deal with a US publisher using his own contacts. As a postscript to this story, it eventually turned out that sales in North America were minimal, so that chasing this market was nothing more than an expensive distraction.

Almost a year after *Motorcycle Voyager* was launched, finances looked as dire as ever. Despite a steady increase in advertising revenue and a big decrease in costs, the magazine was still making a loss, and it was all down to circulation. It wasn't just that we were only selling around 5,000 copies per issue, it was the fact that this represented too small a proportion of the total number printed. In simple terms, the magazine's sales were nowhere near covering its production and print costs, and ad sales couldn't make up the difference. This meant we were heading for a cash crisis – more money had to be found from somewhere because Chris couldn't bail out the company from his own pocket forever. The answer the directors came up with was to secure a business loan of £67,000 through the Small Firms Loan Guarantee Scheme. The plan was to get this money as soon as possible – it was believed it would only take a few weeks – and then use it to keep the magazine going until some other funding source, such as investors, could be found. Saying that, when at this time I enquired about buying equity in Motorcycle Voyager Ltd myself, I was turned down without even being asked what my offer would be. The reason given for this was that, despite being a minority shareholder, I'd hold the balance of power, given that Lolly and Chris had a virtually equal share of the company.

My motivation for wanting to become a shareholder was that I could see a way in which the company might soon become profitable, if and when the sizable loan came through. And despite being turned down as an investor, I soon shared my big insight with Chris: the magazine should go from being bi-monthly (i.e. printed every other month) to monthly.

The reasoning went like this: advertising revenue per issue was growing thanks to Steve's hard work, so the more issues we printed the more ad revenue we'd receive. Being a monthly would also make better use of the company's resources, with its two employees – me and Steve – putting together twice as many issues. It would also make readers less likely to forget about the magazine, as I was sure happened in the two long months they currently had to wait between issues. Retailers and advertisers would probably take us more seriously, too.

But the move to being a monthly would only work if we increased circulation, so that we weren't making a loss with each issue, and this was where the business loan came in. It would be used to both market the magazine and improve distribution, so that it was available in more outlets. When I put these arguments to Chris, he was quickly convinced – *Motorcycle Voyager* would be going monthly.

With surprising dynamism, Laurence researched ways to improve distribution, including paying hefty fees to retailers to ensure the magazine appeared on their shelves. But what neither he nor Chris ever did was put as much thought into marketing the magazine. Even over a year after its launch, I still very rarely met bikers who knew about *Motorcycle Voyager* (although when they saw it most were impressed and wanted to buy it). This clearly illustrated that there was still a lot of work to be done in raising awareness within our market. The directors were well aware of their shortcomings as marketers, but they never tried to overcome these by finding people who would know how to market the publication. Looking back, I can only think that their costly experience with the North America consultants had made them shy about looking for outside help.

In any event, instead of a few weeks, it took three months for the business loan to arrive. By this time the company's debts had grown enormously, so that a large slice of the cash went on overdue invoices, with the balance used to improve distribution. On its own, this didn't increase sales significantly so that each issue, of which there were now twice as many, still made a loss. Yet more money was needed to keep the magazine going, and Chris believed he knew how to get it.

Chris had an associate in the USA who was in contact with a group of Canadians willing to invest over £100,000 in Motorcycle Voyager Ltd. This was the kind of money that could really turn the business around, and the company continued trading on the basis that it would be coming in fairly soon. In fact, such was their optimism the directors even hired a sales assistant for Steve – thereby increasing the company's overheads. But when money again started to get tight the investment from the mysterious Canadians failed to materialise – things were now looking desperate for the company.

Faced with the prospect of losing his entire investment in Motorcycle Voyager Ltd – which amounted to his life savings – Laurence Turner finally decided to take the initiative in finding funding for the company. This included putting together a business plan, at long last, and desperately emailing it off to every venture capitalist he could find, in the hope that a lifesaving sum of money could be raised in the following few weeks. But it was all too little too late, and in September 2004 the company was forced to cease trading, little more than two years after I'd joined. But this wasn't quite the end for the magazine, with the title (but not the company) being bought by another publisher on condition he take on its existing subscribers. However, the new publisher lost interest in the magazine after two issues: it was finally game over for *Motorcycle Voyager*.

Final reckoning

It is interesting to see that there were a number of common factors leading to the failure of both *IT Marketing* and *Motorcycle Voyager* – both of which were great products that deserved to succeed. In each case, a lack of funds hampered development of the magazine so that it might eventually achieve profitability. Or put another way, there was over-optimism as to how quickly – and therefore how cheaply – each would become profitable. In addition, each would probably have benefited from having additional investors with experience of publishing. And both suffered from a lack of planning regarding advertising sales, with hasty and unwise recruitment choices.

But with *Motorcycle Voyager* further factors came into play. There was complacency in the early days which led to poor (and costly) supplier choices and a general underestimation of the task in hand. Then there was the managers' inability to learn from their mistakes, a problem that coaching, mentoring or action learning might have helped solve. And perhaps the directors should have been more realistic about their abilities, and chosen their roles in the company appropriately. In particular, instead of being CEO, publisher and sales director, I believe Laurence should have taken a non-executive role, even though the magazine was his idea. This would have allowed him to concentrate on what he did best, providing ideas for articles and acting as a front man at public events. In turn, an experienced publisher should have been taken on, perhaps as a shareholder (something I'm sure Toby Chapman-Dawe would have recommended). While this would increase the start-up cost for the magazine, it should very soon have paid for itself. For example, this individual would hopefully have taken more control over distribution, so that a higher percentage of magazines ended up on shelves rather than gathering dust in a warehouse. This alone would have justified their salary.

When Motorcycle Voyager Ltd was put into liquidation in August 2005, the Official Receiver reported it had debts of £412,463. This included £196,717 in directors' loans to the company, their initial £50,000 investment, £64,000 remaining on the business loan, and £61,000 owed to suppliers. All of which is pretty amazing, when you think that Chris and Laurence thought it would only take around 25 grand each to successfully set up and run the business. Live and learn, eh?

13

As Your Company Grows

Now we will look at the issues likely to crop up as your business becomes more established. Whether it has made an immediate profit or is still struggling to break even, there are a host of Stupid Factors which lie in wait after you've launched. These can stem from desperation, greed or expedience, not to mention good old ignorance, blind faith and complacency. If you are still trading after two years you are doing well, but it is no time to let your guard down – success in business is all about being prepared for the long haul.

⚠ Now the money is coming in I can finally reward myself.

Having gone to all the trouble of setting up your business, and perhaps getting by on little or no salary, it's only fair to finally get some recompense for your effort and sacrifice. But in business, fairness has little to do with anything; if your company still needs every penny it can get to continue developing, then you can't starve it of cash just because you feel it's time for a reward. Taking money out too soon can quickly lead to stagnation or even failure (as your accountant should be more than happy to point out). Suddenly that £10,000 bonus you gave yourself may not have been much of a reward after all, if it sees your company going bust a few months later.

A desire to get some sort of payback can be particularly strong in entrepreneurs who have finally all but secured big investment funding, after years of scraping by. Except that investors want to see their money building the business, not paying for a bigger house for you. Demands for big pay increases often put off potential investors, or incur their displeasure if they have already put money into your venture. Just as investors may have to wait five years or more to see a return on their capital, so you may have to wait equally long before you get the rewards you so justly deserve.

⚠ I've proven I'm a good business person, so now I can make any business work.

It's easy to believe you have a gift for business if your first venture gets off to a great start. This, in turn, can lead you to consider starting another company before you have fully developed and sold on your existing one – all you need do is take your pick of the business areas you fancy (and not necessarily what you have experience in) and make it happen. And it may well be that you are very capable and can run multiple businesses at once, but before you go from managing a garage to also being a restaurateur, here are a few risk factors for you to consider.

Firstly, try to look as dispassionately as you can and decide, were you truly very skilful with your first start-up or were you just lucky? Of course, everyone needs a certain amount of luck to succeed with a new business, but were there moments when you made bad decisions and succumbed to Stupid Factors, but got away with it? Perhaps you hired the first person to come through your door for a key position and it just so happened he was perfect. This may mean you are a brilliant judge of character, or a lazy chancer who got away with a rash decision. If it's more a case of the latter, then you may be better off sticking with what you already have for the time being.

Also, have you forgotten the hard slog needed to get your business going? Perhaps you didn't get everything right first time, and this caused serious problems, but by working long hours you overcame these setbacks. That's all very well, and may indicate you are indeed an effective business person, but it could have worrying implications. You may find yourself working very hard at your new start-up (because you don't get everything right first time), which will cut into the time you have to manage your original business so that it stops making a profit.

Or perhaps you don't appreciate the crucial role you still play with your first company. Spreading yourself thin between two companies – so that you are not always on the spot to make day-to-day decisions

– could lead to serious problems. Crippling one business in order to set up another is hardly the mark of a gifted entrepreneur.

⚠ This new opportunity is a quick way to make some extra money until the core business takes off.

As a basic principle, when you are developing a new business you should avoid distractions as much as possible. So if a 'new opportunity' is totally unrelated to your start-up's main activity, or only vaguely associated with it, you need to be careful.

Launching and growing a start-up will take up all the energy and commitment you have. Anything that diverts you away from this could have very negative consequences in the long run, even if it makes you a quick buck in the short term. Having said that, something that can bring urgent relief to your cashflow could make the difference between success and failure. You therefore need to think hard about the real value you will get from peripheral activities and whether some other solution, such as outside investment, might not be more appropriate. Certainly, investors themselves will be more interested in a company where management is solely focussed on running the core business.

You should also look at your fundamental motivation for getting involved in other activities early in your start-up's life. Is it really a clever bit of opportunism to bring in much-needed revenue, or an indication that you are bored or have lost heart with your business? Entrepreneurs can be particularly prone to the latter when things start to get difficult – at these times, new business opportunities can seem particularly attractive. After all, something 'new', by definition, hasn't had time to get into trouble or become a chore to manage. When you feel yourself tempted by fresh horizons it is vital that you step back and get some impartial opinions. Your accountant or mentor will hopefully be able to point out the twists in the logic that leads you to think opening a coffee shop will help your software development business.

⚠ I need to continue making all the decisions if this business is going to keep growing.

When you start your growth company, you may have few employees and possible no senior managers. It's up to you to manage everything that happens and make all the decisions. But as soon as your business starts to grow you should be learning to delegate to your employees. If this isn't happening, ask yourself why. Carrying on with a growth company that has you as the only decision maker (in effect, the only real manager) will soon lead to trouble.

For a start, it will put considerable strain on you personally as you use up every hour in the day running the business. This, in turn, will set a limit to how big the company can grow, as you find yourself bogged down in day-to-day issues rather than thinking strategically about how to further develop your business. And if you are looking to sell your venture at some point, buyers will want to see that the company can function once its founder has taken their money and moved on, which won't be the case if you are the only executive decision maker.

There are several reasons you might find it hard to delegate. Maybe you don't trust your managers to make decisions, in which case you should either try harder to recruit people you can trust or think about providing more training for the ones you already have. Then again, perhaps you don't spend enough time talking and listening to your employees to find out what they are capable of – you may find that they have a greater capacity for initiative and good judgement than you realise.

Maybe you're just a control freak who feels very insecure handing on responsibility. In this case, you need to accept the sort of person you are, recognise what needs to be done for the good of the business, and then find strategies for modifying your behaviour. Research has shown that attempts made by people to radically alter their own behaviour never work, so think instead in terms of small changes. This may mean delegating less crucial decision making initially, so that you can see that the world really doesn't fall apart when you aren't in total control, before moving on to more important stuff.

The bonus from all this delegation should be less stress for you (as you will have fewer decisions to worry about), plus you will be tapping more effectively into the knowledge, experience and talents of your employees. Best of all, when these same employees see your willingness to trust them they will almost certainly do a better job.

Thinking strategically is a luxury I don't have time for – there are too many urgent issues that need dealing with now!

Thinking strategically is a necessity, and not something to be put off into the distant future. If you don't make the time to take a broader view of your business, you could eventually find you have been working very hard doing the wrong things for your company. For example, spending months developing an extensive distribution network for a product that consumers increasingly prefer to purchase directly online could prove a dreadful waste of your time. This could have been avoided by devoting just a day to looking at developments in the marketplace and realising that the future of your business lies in e-commerce and not in high street shops.

You can't rely on the time you need for strategy to appear naturally in the course of running your business – there will always be more pressing matters that need dealing with. Therefore, you need to plan an opportunity for strategic thinking.

 This consultant is using lots of fancy lingo, so he must be telling the truth when he says he can make my business more successful – he's hired!

Very broadly speaking, there are two kinds of consultants you are likely to come across as your business develops. There are those who provide specialist knowledge or skill, generally relating to a specific industry. Then there are management consultants, who provide a more general service that can, supposedly, help almost any business function better. Both types have the potential to benefit your company, but in either case extreme caution must be taken before hiring them. The old adage that a consultant is someone who borrows your watch to tell you what the time is, too often proves depressingly true. Certainly, don't let a smooth talker in a slick suit who uses lots of technical language or exotic business-speak to explain how they are going to double your turnover in six months, push you into acting hastily.

Before even talking to a consultant, write down in precise terms what you consider your problems to be and look at the full range of possible solutions. For example, if you have a problem with your computers, getting a service contract with an IT support company may make more sense than hiring an IT consultant to come into the office for a few days to wave a magic wand.

After this exercise, if use of a consultant still looks like a sensible option, then think exactly what the consultant needs to be able to do (in the same way you would plan for taking on an employee), a timescale for their work and a budget. Now you can start talking to several consultants, giving each the same specification for the work that needs doing. (Like any other purchase, approach multiple 'suppliers' to get the best deal, and beware of consultants who approach you first.) You should be looking for solid evidence that they have the knowledge and skill needed to handle your particular problem, as well as references from their clients.

Once you have found a consultant who meets your criteria, draw up a contract with clear terms and conditions before any work begins. This contract should define what exactly you want the consultant to do and what end product there must be from their work. You might also want to state what would not be considered adequate solutions to your problem. For example, spending £10,000 on marketing consultancy to increase your sales, simply to get a two-page report telling you to hire another salesperson and spend £2,000 improving your website, could prove very disappointing.

It's also well worth including: a tough confidentiality clause; a prohibition on working for competitors while working for you, and for a set period afterwards; a stipulation for all your documents and other materials to be returned upon completion; and a confirmation that you will possess the intellectual property rights to anything created for you by the consultant. If you don't want the consultant to publicise the fact that they are working for you, be sure to include a clause preventing that.

There should be a precise definition of what the cost will be. This must be more than just an hourly, weekly or monthly rate, which can leave you wide open to an enormous and unpredictable bill (especially if it isn't made clear when the consultant's clock starts ticking and when it is turned off). Instead, you need to set a maximum figure for what can be charged. In this way you can keep the same level of control over cost as you would with any other supplier. If any consultant resists a contract which caps what they can charge, do not use them.

Prof Birchall says:

As has already been stated, coaching can provide major benefits for business leaders in general and new entrepreneurs in particular. It provides an opportunity for them to reflect and think through why they do the things they do in their businesses; it's also a chance to get off their tracks and look at things differently. A consultant, however, will often tell you how to do something without looking at the particular context of your business. This makes what they do less effective than using coaching, mentoring and similar techniques to solve your problems. Moreover, managers need to be into serial problem solving, which is best achieved through coaching, not consultancy.

Many consultants are self-opinionated and see themselves as the experts – after all, they reason, that's why you've employed them – so they feel impelled to provide a definitive solution to your problem. But there is rarely only one right answer in business. Working with your investors (particularly business angels), a coach and your accountant can, therefore, be a helpful and cheaper alternative, bringing a range of possible solutions.

The simplest way to grow is to buy another company.

On paper, mergers and acquisitions are often very tempting as they allow you to expand your business very quickly. Plus, you may see synergies – ways that the two companies can work together to provide an extra boost to overall profitability – that should more than make up for the costs involved.

However, surveys have shown that, time and again, M&As don't bring the benefits, including increased profits, that were expected.

This is because welding two different companies together, with different systems and cultures, is usually far more difficult than managers expect. Indeed, in the effort and excitement of pulling off the deal, the CEOs may completely forget about how exactly they will make the two businesses work together as one. The end result is that the hoped-for synergies don't materialise, so that a lot of money has been spent with not much to show for it. M&As can present as much of a challenge as choosing to grow organically.

When to go public

If you have been financed by venture capitalists, this may be something you have no control over, as they usually call the shots on a public flotation. Otherwise, only do so when the stock market is high, so that you will get a good price per share. This means delaying your IPO (initial public offering) if the markets have just crashed and acting quickly when they appear to be peaking. In addition, you should be making a profit and enjoying strong sales growth, as these factors will push up your company's valuation.

You must also think whether you really want to turn your start-up into a public company. Becoming a plc will burden you with extra responsibilities, particularly towards the investors to keep the share price high, so that you may no longer feel as free to do as you wish with the business. Anita Roddick makes it no secret that she believes floating The Body Shop was a mistake as it took away the founders' control over the business, including its commitment to ethical trading. However, other successful entrepreneurs, especially in the technology sector, say they wish they'd floated sooner, as going public provided many more opportunities for their business (not to mention making them very rich).

 I can easily expand through franchising.

Franchising can certainly be a very successful way to grow a company, transforming what could be just another lifestyle business into a high-growth operation seemingly overnight. Its many advantages include not having to find plenty of extra capital (effectively, the franchisees are supplying this) and having highly motivated owner/managers working hard to make you rich (rather than dull-eyed, lacklustre employees). However, setting up a reputable franchise is not an easy option. It removes some of the hassles associated with expansion, but only to replace them with new ones. In particular, you will now be required to both establish and, crucially, support a network of franchisees, something you and your management team may have no experience of.

Barriers to growth

Stupid Factor is mostly about getting your venture going and putting you on the path to growth – even if yours is a lifestyle business. But it's worth having a final thought about some of the barriers to revenue growth, which can cause your business to stagnate. A business that fails to achieve its growth potential can be almost as much a failure as one that goes bust. This would be the case if your company, after several years, failed to bring you the level of income you required, so that you were forced to close it (possibly with the loss of your initial investment) and go back to full-time employment. If a business failed to deliver a level of return superior to a far more secure form of investment, for many people – particularly your backers - that too would have to be seen as failure. Growth is not just the icing on the cake when getting a business started, it's one of the main objectives.

A less obvious barrier to growth is the loss of key personnel when you need them the most (as many a manager would say, it's always the good ones that leave first), so you should try hard to make this less likely to happen. And when you do lose a crucial employee, have a Plan B ready for coping until a suitable replacement is found.

Your personal circumstances can also have an important effect on growth. After three years of being in the office more

---

than in the home, your partner may become resentful, so don't neglect this part of your life. A good work/life balance is as important for your business as it is for you.

Prof Birchall says:

Many of the barriers to progress are what I term 'people barriers'. Top of the list is you and your ambition – are you looking for more than just a lifestyle business? This is followed by the quality of leadership in your start-up – you need to quickly and successfully master many different business areas (marketing, finance, etc) without necessarily getting sucked into dealing with too much detail. At the same time, it is vital for entrepreneurs to become aware of the limits of their capabilities – which includes knowing when to step aside and pass on the baton to professional managers. Founders of hi-techs, which are often spun out from universities by good entrepreneurs with great ideas, have a particular problem with hanging on too long. Instead of accepting the limits of their leadership capabilities, they get seduced by the idea that they are going to make it by staying at the helm. They may still make lots of money, but not as much as they might have done had they delegated more to people with the necessary managerial and business communications skills (which entrepreneurs all too often lack).

Outside investors will be able to help founders recognise their managerial shortcomings so that they can, in turn, gather around them people with the abilities they lack. But what if you aren't yet making a profit and don't have the resources to hire the brightest and the best? In this case, you will need to work on improving your own management and leadership skills. Henley doesn't advocate going on formal training courses to do this; in any case, these rarely appeal to entrepreneurs. Instead, our approach when working with SMEs is to provide Just In Time training, whereby immediate access is provided to the training resources which will best help a firm deal with an immediate business problem. Also, as previously described, there is much benefit to be gained from action learning, including the opportunity to network and avoid becoming isolated. Incidentally, don't see networking as a chance to cry on someone's shoulder, but rather as an opportunity to pick up new ideas, assess them, see what relevance they have for you and then take action. Typically, start-ups are 'one idea' businesses. This means the emphasis has to be on coming up with lots of small innovations to aid the really big one, so that it works as cost effectively as possible. Networking, coaching and similar activities are ideal ways to find those small, but very important, innovations that will allow your business to grow and succeed.

14

Further Information

Websites

millionbusinesstips.com

Created in association with *Stupid Factor*, this site is a place for you to pick up smart ideas for running your business, courtesy of fellow entrepreneurs. It also provides an opportunity for you to share your business wisdom by leaving tips of your own. You can even raise the profile of your company by submitting a website link to millionbusinesstips.com. In addition, there are ideas for marketing a small business and links to organisations that can help your company grow.

businesslink.co.uk

Don't even think about starting up without visiting here first. This UK government website is packed full of practical information specifically for people going into business. You can get up-to-the minute information on business regulations, VAT, corporation tax, exporting and much more. You can also find details of your local Business Link.

www.acas.org.uk

This is a great place to get informed about all aspects of employment. A quick visit here could help you avoid falling fowl of the latest legislation as you manage your workforce.

www.statistics.gov.uk

Set up by the UK government's Office for National Statistics, this site is a great place to start your market research, whatever kind of business you have in mind. Along with the sort of headline-grabbing numbers you might expect (inflation rate, unemployment rate, birth rate, GDP, etc.) there's also lots of stats relating to specific business areas. For example, if you want to know the number of UK adults accessing the Internet from home you can find out here. You can also get population and economic details on a particular neighbourhood – gasp in amazement as you discover your new shop will be in the 20,275th most deprived area in England.

Film

Startup.com (2001)

This fly-on-the-wall documentary provides a powerful and very entertaining insight into what it's like to set up and run a high-growth business. How many Stupid Factors can you identify as the founders of US company govWorks.com see their hi-tech dreams descend into old school nightmare? If nothing else, this film brilliantly illustrates that energy, enthusiasm and gritty determination do not, by themselves, guarantee success.

Appendix 1
Business Plan Outline

To get you started, here is a suggested outline for a business plan. It is by no means definitive – it isn't the only way to structure a business plan, and you will almost certainly need to amend it for your particular requirements. But it should at least help make sure your first draft covers all the key areas. You should also refer to the comments made in the main text of *Stupid Factor* regarding writing your business plan.

Cover page
- State the business's name, the authors of the business plan and the date of its completion.

Contents

Executive summary
- This is particularly important if you are seeking outside investment or a loan. It must be no more than two pages and has to make it clear what is special about your business and why someone should want to invest in it. Include key financials here – capital requirement, annual revenues and profit, and the expected return on any equity investment.

Business description
- Say what your business will be about, and include your mission statement and any particular goals or objectives.
- Explain how the business will make money.
- Highlight any strategic assets it already has, such as intellectual property rights or trophy customers.
- Explain your capital requirements, including how the money will be used.
- Explain the 'exit' for an investor, including the likely return on their investment.

Products and services
- Describe in detail what your business will be selling.

Marketing plan
- Provide an overview of your market.
- Explain how you will market your company's products and services, making reference to your market research.
- Identify niche markets where you expect to dominate.
- Highlight your USPs.
- Identify your competitors and how you will overcome them.

Operational plan
- Explain what is involved in setting up your business and include a timetable of activities.
- Provide details of how your business will operate day-to-day.
- Say where your business will be located and why.
- Name any key suppliers and how you will work with them.

Management and organisation
- List the founders of the company, giving appropriate background details.
- List the management team, including key employees, non-executive directors, chairman, mentors and others already committed to the venture.
- Itemise your employee requirements, along with your approach to their recruitment and management.

Financial plan
- This is where you include all the fun stuff: an assessment of start-up capital requirements, revenue projections, costs, breakeven analysis and cashflow projections. (Okay, maybe that's not everyone's idea of fun.)

Appendices
- Documentation to support any assertions made in the main text of the business plan.

Appendix 2
Employment Contracts and Employee Handbook

This example employment contract has the bare minimum of points that should be covered by such a document. Consult with a solicitor or HR professional when drawing up your own employment contracts and employee handbook to make sure you include additional elements relevant to your particular business.

This appendix is kindly provided courtesy of law firm Withy King (www.withyking.co.uk).

EMPLOYER'S NAME AND ADDRESS   EMPLOYEE'S NAME AND ADDRESS

1. Commencement of employment   Your employment commences on [   ]

2. Trial Period *(state length)*   The first [   ] months of your employment will be probationary. Your employment may be terminated on one week's notice during or at the end of the trial period.

3. Place(s) of work *(state 'place or various places')*

4. JOB TITLE *(State title of job)*   Your job title is [   ].

5. REMUNERATION *(State any terms* You will be paid £   per [   ] on or by [   ]. *of rate of remuneration and the intervals at which remuneration is paid)*

6. HOURS OF WORK *(State terms* Your normal hours of work are [   ]. *relating to hours of work, including* You agree that the maximum average week of 48 hours *any terms and conditions relating* under regulation 4 of the Working Time Regulations *to normal hours of work)* 1998 does not apply to you.

7. HOLIDAYS *(State holidays and* You are entitled to [   ] weeks' paid holiday per year *whether inclusive/exclusive of public* [inclusive/exclusive] of public holidays. *holidays, and holiday pay and* The holiday year runs from [   ] to [   ]. *method of calculation of pay including on termination)*

8. SICKNESS/INJURY *(State terms* Statutory Sick Pay will be paid in accordance *relating to incapacity for work* with current legislation. *including sick pay)*

9. PENSION AGREEMENTS *(State any terms and conditions relating to pensions or location of document which gives particulars)*

A designated stakeholder pension scheme is available for you to join after [ ] months continuous employment. The details of the scheme are available from [name]. You agree that representatives of the scheme shall confidentially have reasonable access to personal details held by the firm about you solely for the purpose of supplying you with information about the scheme. There is no contracting-out certificate relating to SERPS.

10. NOTICE *(State periods of notice (1) which the employee is required to give to terminate the contract and (2) which he is entitled to receive from the employer)* :

(1) Employee's notice: (2) Employer's notice
[ ] weeks [ ] weeks
Plus 1 week for each complete year worked.
We reserve the right to pay your basic salary in lieu of notice and to dismiss you without notice or pay in lieu of notice if guilty of gross misconduct.

11. DISCIPLINARY AND DISMISSAL RULES, AND GRIEVANCE PROCEDURES

Our grievance, disciplinary and dismissal procedures (available from [ ]) apply to you. They are discretionary and they do not form part of the terms and conditions of your employment. Your statutory rights are not affected by these procedures.

12. COLLECTIVE AGREEMENTS

There are no collective agreements which affect your employment.

13. CHANGES

We reserve the right to make reasonable changes to your terms and conditions of employment and we will within 1 month after the change(s) provide written particulars thereof.

Signed (Employer)Date   Signed (Employee)Date

NOTES TO EMPLOYEE

1. Commencement of Employment

There is no period of service with another employer which counts towards your continuous service.

2. Place of Work

We reserve the right to change your place of work.

3. Job title

Your job title conveys the nature of the work you are required to perform, but does not limit your duties. You will be expected to carry out such other duties as may reasonably be required.

4. Remuneration

4.1 Payment for work outside the normal hours stated in the attached Written Statement of Terms and Conditions will be at the rates agreed at the time.

4.2 We reserve the right to deduct sums owed by you from your pay or other monies owing.

5. Hours of Work

5.1 The hours of work stated in the attached Written Statement of Terms and Conditions are your normal working hours. You are expected to agree to any reasonable request to work outside your normal hours, or for the proper performance of your duties.

5.2 In the event of work shortage or other circumstances beyond the control of the Employer which prevents normal working, we reserve the right to lay you off or impose short-term working with payment at our discretion subject to current legislation.

6. Holidays

6.1 Holidays must be taken during the holiday year. Holiday cannot be carried forward to the next holiday year.

6.2 On termination of your employment, a payment in lieu of untaken holidays will be made. In the event that you have taken more holiday than has accrued to you by the date you leave, your pay will be reduced proportionately.

7. Sickness and Injury

7.1 Sickness or injury absence must be reported at once.

7.2 On return to work, you must complete a self-certification form.

7.3 If your absence lasts more than 7 days you must provide a medical certificate to cover this and any further period of absence.

7.4 You agree to be examined by a medical practitioner and to disclose the report for the purpose of determining your ability to perform your duties.

7.5 If you are absent for more than 13 weeks in any period of 12 months, we will be entitled to terminate your employment.

Employment contract – some additional elements you might include

- Restrictions on future employment
- Non poaching of staff or customers after end of employment
- Confidentiality
- Details of other benefits given (health insurance, bonus, commission, company car)
- Whole time and attention
- Health and Safety issues
- Expenses
- Share options
- Protection of intellectual property
- Garden leave
- Pay in lieu of notice

- Overtime

Employee handbook (non-contractual) – typical subjects to include

- Disciplinary, dismissal and grievance procedures
- Stress
- Health and Safety
- Equal opportunities
- Harassment and bullying
- Staff development and appraisals
- Public Interest Disclosure (whistle blowing procedures)
- Conduct and standards of behaviour
- Guidance on absences, holidays, time off for family emergencies, etc.
- Company sick pay
- Drugs and alcohol
- Car and other vehicle use
- Data protection
- Email and Internet use
- Redundancy
- Maternity and paternity
- Stop and search (note: to search someone without their agreement is illegal!)

Appendix 3

Checklist of points to be considered before sending a commercial message to a potential customer

This checklist is kindly provided courtesy of Clark Holt commercial solicitors (www.clarkholt.co.uk).

1. Is the data you hold about the potential customer necessary for your legitimate business activities? (Paragraph 6(1), Schedule 2, Data Protection Act 1998). Your 'legitimate business activities' must be balanced against their rights and freedoms.

2. Has the potential customer registered under the Mailing Preference Service, Telephone Preference Service (which now applies to businesses) or Fax Preference Service? (Note that the Mailing Preference Service only applies to individuals, sole traders and partnerships.)

3. Has the potential customer previously given you notice that they do not wish to receive direct marketing from you? (Section 11 Data Protection Act 1998).

4. If your message is electronic (email or text)

    4.1 is there an existing relationship between you and the potential customer or have they given their prior consent to your contacting them in this way? (This is essential under Article 13 of the Directive on Privacy and Electronic Communications and clause 43.4 (c) of the British Code of Advertising, Sale Promotion and Direct Marketing)

    4.2 do all of your messages to the potential customer contain an opportunity for him or her to opt out easily from any further contact from you? (Article 13 of the Directive on Privacy and Electronic Communication)

4.3 does the message make it clear that it is a commercial communication and on whose behalf it is being sent? (Regulation 7, E-commerce Regulations 2002)

4.4 if your message contains a cookie, have you made the recipient aware of this and explained the function of the cookie to them? (Article 5(3) of the Directive on Privacy and Electronic Communication)

4.5 if your message offers electronic contracting, does your message contain your name, address, email address and VAT number, clear indications of prices and details of any trade organisation to which you belong? (Regulation 6, E-commerce Regulations 2002)

4.6 if your message offers electronic contracting, have you provided a clear description of the technical steps required to enter into the contract, how potential customers may correct any inputting errors and how they can access and store the terms of the contract made? (Regulation 9, E-commerce Regulations 2002).

5. If your message to the potential customer is not electronic have you provided him or her with an opportunity to opt out from any further contact from you? (There is no legal obligation for this but it is good practice.)

6. If your message offers to sell goods or services to potential consumers over a distance (e.g. via the Internet, telephone or by catalogue, letter or press advertisement) have they been provided with the following information before any contract is made:

   6.1 your name and your geographical (rather than just an Internet) address

   6.2 a description of the goods or services

   6.3 the period that the offer remains open

6.4 the price (including all taxes and delivery charges)

6.5 the right to withdraw within seven working days

6.6 the arrangements for delivery of any goods? (Regulation 7, Distance Selling Regulations 2000).

7. Does your message comply with the regulations of the British Code of Advertising, Sale Promotion and Direct Marketing? (The 11th edition came into force on 4 March 2003.)